one honest woman

Copyright © 2018 by Dannie Lynn Fountain
All Rights Reserved

Published in the United States by Side Hustle Press

ISBN: 978-0-9993199-1-8

Printed in the United States of America

Edited by Jodi Brandon of Jodi Brandon Editorial
Book cover design by Ari Krzyzek of Chykalophia

For inquiries on speaking engagements, bulk orders, and more, please visit: www.danniefountain.com

*to anyone who thinks their
experience wasn't "bad enough"
to qualify as meaningful,
this book is for you.*

Contents

Author's Note 7

Foreword: Masterful Escape Artists. 11

A Calibration. 17

Why "One Honest Woman"? 23

Little Elephant Wrangler. 31

Don't Ask Me to Multiply 39

A Fish out of Water. 47

Playing Soldier 55

Not My Proudest Moment 69

Science Is Creative 75

The Loss of a Mother 81

Heart on a Sleeve 97

A Childhood of Loss 105

Agitating and Tumbling 115

Thrice Fired. 121

Girls, Girls, Girls 135

The Girl Without a Home 145

I Love Lamp. 161

Accidental Googler. 181

So What's Next? 189

Acknowledgments 195

About the Author .201

Author's Note

I never planned to write a book about myself. I always said I didn't have enough of a story to tell to fill a compelling number of pages. My life story requires that one suspend disbelief; it rests safely nestled between absolute insanity and plausible deniability. Yet here we are.

The stories contained herein are told to the best of my knowledge and memory. Names are changed to protect the guilty (unless the guilty have given permission to be thusly exposed, in which case they are at your mercy, dear readers. Play nice.).

The stories contained herein are also only a slice of my life (and there wasn't time or space to include *all* that has happened so far). As of this writing, I sit tenderly filled with the hopeful potential of more years left to live than those lived thus far. I have not yet learned all of life's lessons, nor do I pretend to be omnipotent, psychic, or any other form of a know-it-all. This book is not meant to be used as a guide for life and is written for entertainment purposes first. God save the person who derives actionable advice from the life I've lived.

Now that I've included far too much language to disclaim away any responsibility I might have for how you interpret the words within, let's get on with the show.

foreword

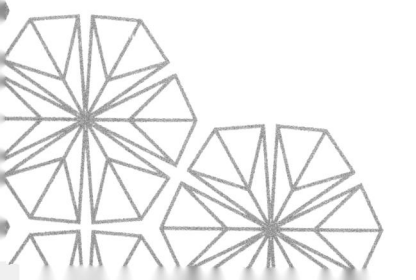

FOREWORD

Masterful Escape Artists

We sat at the table, her eyes meeting mine when I asked her, "What is it that you're running from?"

It hit me then that we were all running: from our pasts, from the mistakes we've made or the things that have happened to us.

We're running from the person we've become, from the fact that we aren't where we thought we would be.

We're running so hard that sometimes it hurts more to stay still than to keep putting one tired, weary foot in front of the other.

We've become masterful escape artists looking for our next blinking red "exit" sign—but what would happen if we paused, sat, and rested?

These are all questions I asked myself after meeting Dannie Fountain in real life. Within what felt like hours, I went from not knowing Dannie to seeing her everywhere: online, in my inbox, when I opened an app on my phone. There she was, this beautiful woman, opening her life up to the world, but behind the filters, behind the posts, I knew there was a story waiting to be told. One she was likely running from.

So there we sat at the picnic table in the bustling office when I (a mere stranger) called her on it. What happened next wasn't quite what I expected—though looking back, I should have known.

Always an achiever, Dannie set out to prove me wrong. She started sharing more boldly; she didn't book her next wheels-up adventure and camp out, hiding away. She sat in the hard, the messy, and turned it into her message—the message that today, you have the honor of holding in your hands.

Whether you run with it or need space to sit through it, this story is a reflection of not just Dannie's truth but yours, too.

We all have a story, we all are running, but life can change when we learn to sit with what feels unbearable, when we learn to honor the mess, when we learn to share the message. This message just might change your life, like that simple conversation with Dannie changed mine.

Jenna Kutcher

Photographer, educator, host of The Goal Digger Podcast, mac n' cheese lover, passionate marketer, and dear friend

a calibration

A Calibration

One *Honest Woman*. What woman? Why is she honest?

For this book to make sense to you, it might help if you know who I am.

Hi. I'm Dannie. I wrote this book as a 23-year-old woman splitting her time between Chicago, Illinois, and Ann Arbor, Michigan. As you hold it in your hands, I am 24, or maybe a little older.

I'm the oldest child of four by birth and today fall somewhere in the middle of 12 children.

I have a bachelor of arts from Albion College (affectionately called "the Harvard of the Midwest") and a master of science from Indiana Wesleyan University.

I run a freelance marketing firm, speak at conferences across the globe, and have a day job working in marketing for Google.

I honed my professional prowess working in marketing for brands such as Whirlpool and H&R Block, and have a combined nine years' experience as an entrepreneur and strategist.

My work (and the work of teams I've been a part of in my corporate and entrepreneurial careers) has been submitted to and recognized by Cannes Lions, the Effies, CASE, the North American Excellence Awards, the American Advertising Awards, the Shorty Awards, D&AD Impact White Pencil, and more.

The same work has been featured in *Advertising Age*, *Adweek*, *Forbes*, *Holstee Magazine*, *Belong Magazine*, and more.

I have what some would call the oddest list of accomplishments: international science fair finalist, hometown pageant queen, fraternity president, student pilot, and certified scuba diver, to name a few.

I was named Officer of the Year by Civil Air Patrol and the VFW in 2009. I was named Leader of the Year by Omicron Delta Kappa in 2014. And perhaps most importantly, I have kissed a cow. More than once.

introduction

INTRODUCTION

Why "One Honest Woman"?

"It's your turn," they said. I was sitting at Inspired Retreat in fall 2016 when Heather Crabtree turned to me and asked why I hadn't told my story. She'd noticed, in the books that I've edited, that my story was conspicuously missing. She wasn't the first person to mention this (in fact, I'd been told over and over again), nor was she the last, but she was perhaps the person to say it the boldest.

Soon thereafter, I met Jenna Kutcher, a woman I'd looked up to online for ages. I already had a working relationship with her husband, Drew, through his business, The Kutcher Method, but this was my first time meeting Jenna. She was something else, a woman born with a powerful mind for business and a talent for making people feel things. The day we met, I too felt something, and the seed that Heather had boldly planted sprouted its first leaves under the care of Jenna's firm hands.

After sharing the stories of 57 entrepreneurs across all walks of life through *The Side Hustle Gal*, *The Bucketlist Babe*, and *Big Plan for the Creative Mind*, I finally conceded that I need to share my story, too. This journey now continues with this book: *One Honest Woman*.

ABUSED. BEATEN. WELL-TRAVELED. WELL-EDUCATED.

Those four characteristics aren't often all held by the same person; some of them shouldn't have to be held by any person at all. But those four characteristics are the beginning of my story, both as a woman and as an entrepreneur. This isn't your typical business book. This isn't a toolkit to take you to the next level or a road map to your first six-figure month. This is a raw story of guts and courage and what it means to wake up one day and believe you'll come out on the other side. This is the story of getting

One Honest Woman

knocked down and continuing to fight anyway. This is a story of survival.

I've made more mistakes than I can even count throughout my brief years on this planet. This book? It's an homage to those mistakes and a place where I relive them not only for my own healing, but for your growth as well.

Nearly two years ago, I was packing up what was to be my last solo apartment. I'd moved two states away and more than eight hours from home because I'd fallen in love with who I thought was my forever person. We were in the final stages of moving in together.

Little did I know that a week later, I'd come home from the most AMAZING trip overseas to someone I didn't recognize. Someone who was completely NOT in love with me and **saw my business and the fire in my heart for entrepreneurship as things that hindered my ability to be human.** Someone who had felt these feelings for a long time, and hinted at them (amidst my obliviousness), but now was making sure that I was painfully aware of their reality.

As I sit here and reflect on everything that's happened, that breakup was almost a metamorphosis. That life-changing event, no matter how painful, served as the catapult that launched me to where I am today.

On that day two years ago, I couldn't have imagined that I'd be here, standing before you today, as you're holding my story in your hands.

I had no idea that I could be an international speaker, a sought-after marketing strategist, a podcaster, someone who people looked up to, someone who was respected.

I never *dreamed* I would be working for Google, arguably the number-one company in the world.

Back then, my brand wasn't even my name, the idea of nomad life hadn't even crossed my mind, and the concept of charging what I was worth was so foreign to me that my partner was helping me decrease the amount of my quotes because she (and, by proxy, I) believed that I didn't need to be charging that much.

I say all this to tell you that starting over wasn't

easy. Separating my identity from hers, and finding my true self again, was all a fight. I made so many bad decisions in those first few months after we split. I had allowed my worth to be defined by her approval. It took months for me to redefine my worth as something that I owned, and it's still something that I struggle with today. But it was worth the effort.

I need you to understand that this instance was one of many that has changed my life in a marked way.

If you're struggling to see your true self, know that it's okay for you to just begin again, too. Take that first breath, then take the leap.

It's the only way you'll survive.

Follow along as I share the story that brought me to my future—a story of blood, sweat, and tears. This isn't a story for the faint of heart, and it might even make you cry. This is *One Honest Woman.*

little elephant wrangler

THE BEGINNING

Little Elephant Wrangler

My journey began at some point in spring 1993. Given an expected delivery date of December 14th, I began my life with a newfound tradition that I would carry throughout adolescence: to defy expectation. I was born 10 days later, on December 24th, after 36 hours of what I've been told was excruciating labor and one painstaking C-section.

I was born with a full head of jet-black hair; strong, proud lungs (capable of piercing wails); and the big, bold, bubbly personality to match.

A variety of personality tests and ways of sorting yourself have identified that I should (and actually mostly do) possess the following traits:

Faithful, ambitious, self-controlled, determined, responsible, sincere. Also shy, pessimistic, awkward, detached, self-centered, gloomy, stubborn. Steadfast, trustworthy, persistent, composed, self-reliant, constructive, practical, humourous, fearless and stable. Also stubborn, dominant, obstructive, dogmatic, conceited, self-centered, lazy, exacting. Intelligent, reserved, sensitive, picky eater, worrisome, detail-oriented, adaptable, dependable, precise and careful. Also fussy, meticulous, negative, cranky.

My earliest memory came at age three. My grandmother has told me this story a hundred times and I never tire of it. Please indulge me as I recount it here for you.

My grandparents took me to the Shrine Circus a few miles from my childhood home as a treat. I don't remember much from the circus itself, except for the elephants. I've always loved elephants. At the end of the performances, the elephant trainer brought this beautiful creature back into the ring and began giving elephant rides. (At the time, I was not old enough to

One Honest Woman

understand what elephants go through as part of a circus. I now know better.) Knowing what I now know about elephants, this gentle giant was no younger than 60 years, and the wear and tear of a circus life were evident across her skin and in her deep, rich eyes.

After everyone had been granted rides as a group (seven to 10 people on the elephant's back at a time in a large saddle apparatus, one to two laps around the circus arena per ride), people started getting off the elephant's back and saying goodbye. The trainer asked if I would want to ride on my own and my granny said that of course I would! I climbed the ladder and sat atop the elephant on my own: three years old, messy hair, lips and cheeks stained from what I can only guess was a cherry Icee. My granny took a photograph that I still have today, Shrine Circus ticket gently taped to the back, carefully dated with my age at the time, of that exact moment.

After a few short passes back and forth in front of the stands, the trainer gestured for me to climb down, which I did quickly and deftly, proud of my solo elephant rider status. Granny and I giggled together, marveling at the experience, and she turned to me and asked what I thought my mom would think. I said that my mom would have a cow if she knew what we'd done! In that moment I realized I was different from my family. I didn't see the problem with a solo elephant ride, nor was I unaware of the potential danger. I remember being conscious of her power beneath me as she moved and how she seemed tired, yet with this little girl atop her back, this seemed as though it was the brightest moment of her day. (I now realize it was because I was the lightest load she'd probably ever carried.) I didn't understand how my mom wouldn't be able to differentiate between the potential for danger and the controlled situation within which I encountered it.

A couple years later, my grandparents took me to the circus again, this time to see The Flying Wallendas. The family is a group of circus act and daredevil stunt performers, most known for performing highwire acts without a safety net. They also hold more than a couple Guinness World records. Their most famous performance routine was developed by Karl Wallenda and called the seven-person chair pyramid. After performing this routine for a couple decades,

One Honest Woman

while performing at the Michigan State Fair Coliseum in Detroit in January 1962, the front man on the wire (Dieter Schepp) faltered and the pyramid collapsed. Three men fell to the ground and two died. Karl injured his pelvis, and another performer was paralyzed from the waist down. The performance that we attended was the first performance in more than 35 years, since that accident, during which they attempted the seven-person chair pyramid again. Yet another dangerous stunt was observed—and yet another time I considered the realities of humanity. I couldn't help but compare these two experiences and wonder what the future impact would be.

Just shy of 20 years after riding an elephant for the first (and only) time, I found myself in northern Thailand, in the Elephant Nature Park, standing next to a similarly aged elephant. My hand rested gently on her shoulder as we stood side-by-side and I once again recounted this fond memory. Soon thereafter, a gentle giant crossed my path as I wandered the compound and trumpeted proudly less than 5 feet in front of me, stamping her feet on the ground as she called to her young. The ground shook in a way

I won't soon forget: No matter how gentle, giant is giant. Hindsight is 20/20, as they say, as I can now see how this kind of true bravery has served me well throughout my life thus far.

> *there is no "one true way" when it comes to entrepreneurship. what are the characteristics that you uniquely possess that equip you for your entrepreneurial journey?*

don't ask me to multiply

THE BEGINNING

Don't Ask Me to Multiply

I can honestly say that, for better or worse, I was never outwardly the ostracized nerd or the cool, popular kid throughout school, though I can say with certainty that my classmates over the years remember me for one reason or another (not always positively, I admit).

A few years after the elephant adventure, I found myself in second grade. I was attending a private Catholic school, I had awesome friends, and I felt like I belonged. Nobody judged me yet for answering questions right away, and lunch was still a blissful time of playscape wonder.

Second grade was also my first Embarrassing Memory (capitalized to denote the recurrence of this particular kind of memory). I was selected to be the cantor during First Communion. The cantor is "a person who sings solo verses or passages to which the choir or congregation responds," which sounds like an awfully big responsibility for someone who has not yet attained double-digit status in age. I accepted the responsibility with glee and began practicing my music daily.

First Communion Day arrived and we lined up two by two outside the church. We walked inside without error and took our seats near the front of the church. My moment came and I approached the altar, music clutched close to my chest. As I stepped up the first step, my foot caught on my dress. In front of the entire second grade, much of the school, and a litany of proud parents, I fell on my face in a tumble of lace and silk. (I unfortunately was too young for Jennifer Lawrence to have popularized this move, and as a result felt *very* uncool. Perhaps she even got the idea from me!)

Without a single tear, I stood back up, went up the rest of the steps, and finished my cantor responsibilities without further incident. Little did I know this moment would come to be a metaphor for my life.

Soon after First Communion, Miss White pulled my parents aside (unbeknownst to me) and indicated that I might be ready to skip third grade. The next day I was sent to third grade to Mr. Gerhard's class, where I participated in a multiplication drill (and somehow answered problems correctly—a lucky roll of the dice) and started to learn states and capitals. At the end of the day, it was decided that I would skip ahead to fourth grade the next year instead of going to third grade. Don't ask me to multiply or to name states and capitals, because I never properly learned how.

Skipping third grade set me up to be forever ahead of the curve, as far as age goes. It's a fascinating thing, how one choice early on in your life can have far-reaching impacts. As a result of skipping third grade, I started college before I was an "adult," graduated college before I could legally drink, and even started my first corporate job unable to drink at the company Christmas party.

When I was in seventh grade, I was in the robotics club. Our goal was to build robots out of legos and program them to do something incredible. Sarah, my best friend, and I built and programmed our robot to play unbeatable checkers. No matter how good you were at checkers, our robot would beat you every time. We had to learn complex programming (and of course how to build a sturdy robot) and we eventually made it to the Lego Robotics Worlds, where we competed against teams from around the globe. We were in seventh grade, not even teenagers yet, and there we were competing against robot programmers around the world.

I get asked all the time if I think these situations, from competing at the world level as a pre-teen to graduating college before my first legal drink, had an impact on who I am, who I've become. There are two answers to that question.

On the one hand, as this book is published, I am 24. At 24, I have completed undergrad and grad school. I've worked a year in a corporate job, spent two years running my business full-time, and am now approaching a year into another corporate job. I've traveled the world, had whirlwind romances, and experienced profound loss. My age-appropriate peers, however, are one year out of undergrad and in many cases still in grad school. One could argue that I'm set up for success: I could fail miserably today, pick myself up tomorrow, and still have a couple years before I'd be considered "behind" them.

On the other hand, however, there are many challenges to moving through these parts of your life at a younger age. If I choose to date a peer the same age as me, it's likely that they're three to four years behind me in "life stage." There's a vast chasm between those I went to high school with and me as far as where we are in our lives. As a result, many of my friends tend to be seven to 10, if not more, years older.

As I look back on my secondary school years, and even my college years, I largely see a race. I was in a race to finish first—to get there faster than anyone, to "win bigger" than anyone. That race only served to broaden the chasm between my peers and me.

People have often asked me if I thought I'd run out of runway too soon. If you've ever been in a plane, you know that it needs runway and room to accelerate before it takes off. If the runway is too short, it'll crash. If the runway is too long, it might underestimate when to go wheels-up and end up skimming the trees. This metaphor exists for humans, too: too long a runway and we end up coddled and soft; too short a runway and we have the potential to fail hard and fast before we even get off the ground. My runway was shrinking. The more I accomplished, the less there was for me to "do" in each stage of my life.

Looking back now, I was a generalist at life when many of my peers were specialists. I dipped my toes in so many different ponds and experienced so many different things, while my peers devoted themselves wholly to a few special things. Which experience was better? I'm not sure I can say for sure.

> *which experience did you have as a child: generalist or specialist? do you think it impacted how you view the world today?*

a fish out of water
———

LIFE'S LITTLE LESSONS

A Fish out of Water

I've always felt like a fish out of water. A little ahead of or behind the curve. It's no surprise that the sport I chose to pursue throughout my academic career was swimming.

I was on a travel swim league in middle school. It was similar to any other travel sport, with practices five days a week and then meets in different locations within a reasonable driving distance every weekend. In high school, I was on the varsity swim team with five days a week of practice (and two days a week with two-a-days). In an average week in high school, I swam around 10 miles during preseason and closer to 15 during peak season.

My events were the 50 freestyle and the 500 freestyle. The 50 is a fast event; most record-holders swim it in under 23 seconds (my best was 32 seconds). The 500 is a bit more paced event, with record-holders swimming it in a minute and 45 seconds (my best was a minute and 59 seconds).

My high school swimming career was an interesting one, full of highs and lows, but largely positive overall. One of my favorite memories is getting to swim the 500-yard freestyle. This event was nestled safely between two butterfly events, and we only had one or two talented butterflyers on our team. As a result, my performance in the 500 free was always a gamble: Would I intentionally swim it slowly (and get away with it, due to my physical appearance) to give the butterflyers more time to recover between events, or would I swim it at an all-out sprint, hoping to place? My coach would make the call based on the needs of our team during each meet, but it was always an adventure.

Being a plus-size swimmer was one of the best parts of swimming altogether. I was surprisingly afforded the opportunity to be a diver during my final year on the high school team. I'd always looked at the divers with a mix of admiration and longing: wishing I was talented enough to move my body the way theirs moved, and stunned by the strength and control they displayed. When I stepped up onto the diving board for the first time, I was tremendously uncertain. Diving scores are based on a variety of factors, but one of the strongest is precision. Could my curvy-even-then body manage to operate tightly enough to reduce splash and garner decent scores? Most days, I couldn't, but every once in a while I'd perform a dive that amazed even me, garnering high enough scores to actually impact the outcome of the meet.

During chemistry class my junior year of high school, I got a hydrochloric acid burn. I was being careless and spilled the acid on the lab table and it burned my thigh, leaving an open wound. Unfortunately due to the acid being hydro*chloric* acid and me being a swimmer, I had to stay out of the pool during the peak part of the season that year.

This ended up being a blessing in disguise, because my coach put me on a weight-training regimen to maintain the strength in my legs and upper body. By the end of junior year, I was able to complete a one-rep maximum leg press of 500 pounds (significantly higher than the standard leg press amount of 1.8–2.2x your body weight). My upper-body strength at the end of that year was stronger than it has ever been (before or since).

Junior year was also the year I quit the swim team. I wish I could remember the exact circumstances around why I decided to quit, but I do remember this: To get your varsity letter on the swim team, you had to achieve a certain number of points. Placing (1, 2, 3) in a heat was worth X points, and then placing in the overall race (combination of all the heats for that event) was worth more points. At the start of junior year, I hadn't yet earned my varsity letter, but for the first time ever, it was actually in sight. At the team dinner that year, as the varsity letters were handed out, some girls who had swum all three years thus far (freshman–junior) were granted "gratuitous letters"; they hadn't yet attained the point threshold, but for their dedication to the team, they were given a varsity letter. I was not among those girls, although I had participated in not only all three years, but also summer conditioning. I'd also gotten my personal record time down by more than 30 seconds on both of my longer events during the junior year season. I was pissed.

At the first practice following the team dinner, I remained in the locker room. Murmurs echoed around me as girls discussed the events of the night before, most disagreeing with my not having been awarded a varsity letter. They felt this way especially knowing that from time to time I was intentionally throwing my 500-yard free event (at the behest of the coach) to get other girls more rest time, but in doing so was losing out on points and the opportunity to get closer to a varsity letter.

In perhaps one of the most profound experiences of solidarity in my life to date, the team decided that nobody was going to come out of the locker room, in support of the perceived slight at the team awards dinner. About 15 minutes after we should have all been on deck to warm up, the coach walked into the locker room to find out what we were all doing and why we weren't stretching. After hearing our reasons, she asked us all to take seats in the bleachers and said that we'd talk things out. We headed to the bleachers and a heated debate ensued, with neither side listening to the other. I didn't speak much other than to say I was tremendously disappointed, but I was beyond moved by the girls who chose to speak out on my behalf. The coach opted not to grant me a varsity letter, so I walked out of practice that day and was off the team.

All this time, I'd felt like a fish out of water. A little ahead, a little behind, but never just right. My team showed me that day that, actually, I was right where I was meant to be, and they supported me.

> *you don't need to be a part of "the core" to be a part of the group. what are the ways different people in your life overlap and intersect, and how does that enhance or detract from your interpersonal experiences?*

playing soldier

GROWING UP

Playing Soldier

My resume as a child was perhaps the most ridiculous and mixed resume a child could possibly possess. I was involved in everything from Girl Scouts to choir to Civil Air Patrol (CAP). CAP is the auxiliary of the United States Air Force and was born one week prior to the Japanese attack on Pearl Harbor. Its members (like me!) perform three congressionally assigned key missions: emergency services (which includes search and rescue by air and ground and disaster relief operations); aerospace education for youth and the general public; and cadet programs for teenage youth.

In hindsight, Civil Air Patrol was an odd choice

for me. I'm more of a bookworm than a brute, and the thought of me crawling under barbed wire (through mud) makes many of my friends laugh. However, the years spent in CAP were among the most fascinating of my life.

I volunteered from 2005 to 2013 in the Civil Air Patrol, soloing an airplane and earning my scuba diver certification as a result of my membership. I also had the opportunity to refuel an aircraft from the belly of a C-130 Hercules; lobby in Washington on behalf of Civil Air Patrol; visit the Capitol, Supreme Court, State Department, Pentagon, and CIA buildings; and experience so many other life-changing opportunities.

In early 2006, just a few months after joining CAP, I was asked if I wanted to participate in an upcoming drill competition. If you've ever seen *Cadet Kelly*, it's very similar. Groups of teenage youth march in precise and stylized routines and competE for a trophy. The team that reached out to me had won the state-level competition and was going on to regionals at Wright-Patterson Air Force Base in Dayton, Ohio. We didn't end up winning that regional competition, but I will say this: It taught me a lot about what I could

One Honest Woman

endure. I ran an eight-minute mile at that competition. That may not seem very fast to you, but my prior recorded best mile was north of 10 minutes. I also was one of the strongest team members during the Quiz Bowl portion of the competition, despite only having joined CAP six months prior.

In fact, I walked away from the competition with a passion for Quiz Bowl. I later transferred squadrons and championed my new squadron participating in the Academic Bowl competition at the state level. We built out four teams (A, B, C, and D) and put together a studying schedule as well as a competition among the four teams to build out who would belong on each team. Rather than stacking the A team with all our best performers, we spread those performers among the four teams and then focused in on boosting the lagging members' knowledge. Because of this strategy, we walked into the state competition with four very strong teams, two of which placed in the top five and one winning the entire competition.

2006 was also the year that I attended Search and Rescue (SAR) Academy. Whereas Academic

Bowl was an overwhelmingly positive experience, SAR academy was rather the opposite. The premise of SAR academy is nine days and nights in the woods, Army Ranger survival-school style. The program culminates with a three-day/two-night mock rescue mission, including camping out with minimal supplies, 17-mile day hikes, and, of course, rescuing "civilians." I was entirely unprepared and out of shape when I showed up for SAR Academy (and also made the mistake of packing mostly tin can food for while we were at "home base"—which I then had to lug up the hill to even get to home base). I ended up (unsurprisingly) fracturing my growth plate and then hiking on it for two additional days before I got home and in a cast.

At the midpoint of my CAP career, I had the opportunity to pilot a new program: Neutral Buoyancy Lab (NBL). We'd long ironed out experiences for cadets to learn more about air and space, and this was focused on the sea. The "official" NBL is an astronaut training facility and neutral buoyancy pool operated by NASA. Trainees wear suits designed to provide neutral buoyancy to simulate the microgravity that astronauts would experience during spaceflight.

One Honest Woman

CAP's version of NBL is a condensed version of that program ran by a former NASA instructor.

The objectives of the program were simple: (a) get trained in the proper use of scuba gear, (b) work on a series of tasks while submerged underwater, and (c) construct a simulated section of a space station. We also had the opportunity to meet and talk with astronaut Chris Cassidy.

During the final day of NBL, teams had to complete a timed series of exercises, one of which was "rescuing" one of your teammates who was without air. To complete this exercise, after submerging, the instructors would turn off one team member's air supply. After a brief period of time, the air that had already left the tank would run out, and that person would be without oxygen. For my team, I was to be the person without air.

We suited up and got ready to go underwater, but due to a simple mistake, rather than turning my air supply off underwater, my air supply was never turned on. Submerged and aiding in the first exercise, I quickly realized I was without air. If you surfaced mid-competition, your team lost points and you had to sit out the rest of the competition out. I had two choices: surface and sit out the competition (and also render my team unable to complete the "rescue" exercise) *or* hold my breath and hope that we completed the first exercise quickly.

I opted to hold my breath, and luckily we completed the first exercise in about 45 seconds. I signaled to the team that we needed to *hurry* through the rescue exercise and they quickly caught on that I'd been without air the whole time. They cleared my regulator, got my air turned on, and got oxygen flowing again. We were able to complete the remaining exercises (and ended up finishing second overall), but I was haunted the rest of that experience by the no-air moments. After the NBL itself, many of us stayed to complete our scuba diving certification and my first open water dive nearly caused a panic attack, as I was checking my air every five seconds to make sure it was working. (I survived, however, and have since completed nearly 30 dives.)

National Flight Academy was perhaps the single most life-changing moment of my CAP career. After applying for and being awarded the Mary Von Mach scholarship (named for the first licensed female pilot in the state of Michigan), I left for Camp Ashland, Nebraska, to begin flight training. Over the course of a little more than two weeks, I completed all the ground school instruction, necessary training flights, and examinations. As the end of the Academy approached, I began to prepare for my solo flight. The first solo flight is a critical step in flight training: You must complete 10 hours of solo flight to earn a private pilot's certificate, and this flight determines your aptitude to complete those hours.

On the day of my solo flight, I sat out on the tarmac with the other cadets as one by one they attempted their flights. The cadet before me took off with ease, but upon landing nearly stripped the tires on the plane bald due to coming in too hot. If I hadn't been nervous before that moment, I definitely was then.

My solo flight went seamlessly. My time in the air alone was included some of the most terrifying and yet peaceful moments of my life. I came back down to the ground and upon graduation received my solo wings, one of my prized possessions to this day.

Soloing wasn't the only terrifying experience I had while at NFA. Another was refueling an aircraft from the belly of a C-130 Hercules. Nothing like laying on your stomach while 25 feet away an aircraft is getting refueled in midair, all while you're looking out the opening down to the ground a few thousand miles below.

After transferring to a new squadron, I had the opportunity to join a color guard unit. Color guard is the four-person unit responsible for carrying the flags in formal ceremonies and parades. Just like drill team, CAP holds annual competitions for color guards across the country. The color guard unit I was a part of also had the opportunity to compete at the wing and regional color guard competitions. However the coolest experience we had was getting to present the colors at one of the 2009 NCAA Men's Final Four competitions in Detroit.

In what would have been the defining moment of my CAP career, in 2011 I applied to attend the International Air Cadet Exchange (IACE).

One Honest Woman

Cadets from programs like CAP all over the globe exchange places for nearly a month, experiencing life in the other country and learning more about its history and military. My application was accepted, and I was all set to attend, until I separated from my family that March and my birth mother refused to sign the paperwork allowing then-17-year-old me to travel abroad. I didn't end up going.

Even though I didn't participate in IACE that year, something tremendous came out of that experience: I met Carsen. Of the 56,000 then-members of Civil Air Patrol, Carsen and I were two of the five American cadets randomly accepted and slotted to go to Turkey. We connected online as preparations for the trip were underway and soon learned a very unique fact about one another: We were born on the same day, within mere hours of each other, on opposite sides of the country.

Carsen and I never ended up meeting (and to this day have never met face to face), but over the past seven years have remained in touch, affectionately referring to one another as "twins." I went on to go to Albion and then pursue the career you've begun to hear about in this book. Carsen went to college, participated in ROTC, and now serves as a pilot in the US Air Force. Though I never went to Turkey that year, it was very much a "right place, right time" moment, and Carsen's and my lives became intertwined. We'll often accidentally end up in the same city, one leaving hours before the other arrives. It's not my place to tell his story, but in many ways, we've been through similar struggles and triumphs side by side, connected by an invisible thread.

While I wouldn't trade my Civil Air Patrol experience for the world, it also gives me mixed feelings. I have siblings in the service, and many of my closest friends either are serving or have served. My patriotism and national pride run strong, even as a first-generation American-born individual, even in the current state of our world. It feels strange to talk about my time in CAP so proudly. On some level, I contributed to our nation's safety. CAP is, after all, responsible for Congressionally assigned missions, including the vast majority of inland homeland security missions. For example, CAP was one of the first planes to fly over the destroyed World

Trade Center in September 2011. But the reality is that CAP is an auxiliary organization and not "true" military. I grew up playing soldier and was forever changed as a result.

not my proudest moment

———

GROWING UP

Not My Proudest Moment

Say the word *fraternity* and you'll quickly evoke images of campus scandals across the country. However, at my undergrad university, sororities and fraternities were a big deal. Many of the Greek organizations had been on campus for 130+ years, having been founded in the 1870s and '80s. More than half of the campus was Greek as well, making Greek life a great way to make friends.

I opted to rush a sorority during the second semester of my freshman year. The rush process was a three-day weekend, with accepted pledges receiving bids on the third day.

I never thought I would be a sorority girl. I'm not

the usual model: I'm queer, definitely not skinny, definitely not blonde, and I didn't have long hair at the time, either (the norm for sorority girls on my campus).

I pledged Kappa Alpha Theta. Theta was the first Greek-letter fraternity for women (and interestingly was actually called a *fraternity*, not a sorority, due to its "first of its kind" status and the lack of popularization of the word *sorority* at that time). I chose Theta because their values were highest scholarship, the widest influence for good, and a moral standard of love. I believed I was joining an organization that would change me for good. Phi Beta Kappa's first female members were Thetas, Theta was the first sorority established at many of the Ivy Leagues, and there are many notable Thetas worth looking up to: the Bush daughters, Sheryl Crow, the Disney daughters, Tory Burch, a Reagan daughter, Kerri Strug, Elizabeth Warren, Whitney Port, Melinda Gates, Lynne Cheney, and Cindy McCain, to name a few.

My pledging process was pretty standard as far as sorority pledging goes. I completed that, was initiated, and started down the path of being a

One Honest Woman

Theta. I dove head-first into getting involved, participating in Anchor Splash (an annual synchronized swimming competition), A-Chi-Roke (a singing contest to raise money for domestic violence victims), and many other Panhellenic competitions.

The moment when things started to change, however, came when we were standing in a circle after a meeting. These circles were a space in which we could share exciting things that had happened to us. (Many an engagement was announced in this setting.) One week, the exciting information I chose to share was that I was in a new relationship...with a woman. Little did I know that this was a less-than-ideal thing to share.

Over the remainder of that semester, my friendships with members of the sorority started to degrade. At the same time, I took on a leadership role in the sorority as assistant treasurer. Unfortunately, by the time the semester came to an end, it was clear that things weren't going well. You can pause your sorority membership for one semester, so I did precisely that.

At the end of the following semester, it was clear that things weren't going to change. There had been drama within the chapter, among other issues, so I decided to go "early alumni" and no longer be a member of the chapter at my college.

I learned a lot from being in a sorority. In many ways, I agree with the "you pay for your friends" trope. The friendships only started happening once my membership payment came in. Coincidence or not, it was an unfortunate feeling. This wasn't my proudest moment: opting to "pay for friends" and then discovering that even money can't guarantee anything. But lessons learned are lessons learned.

> *there is probably one group of people that you get along with best. who are your "tribe" members, your "wolfpack," the people that have your back no matter what happens? how often do you say thank you to these people and/or show them support in return?*

science
is creative

———

GROWING UP

Science Is Creative

I never was much of a math whiz, but somehow I found myself taking advanced math and science classes in high school. And not just taking advanced classes, but placing third at the Lego Robotics World-level competition and being a finalist at the 2010 International Science and Engineering Fair.

Let me explain.

In ninth grade, I took a test that qualified me for the St. Clair County M.A.S.T.E.R.S. program and to be a student at the Macomb Academy of Arts and Sciences. The former enabled me to go to a two-week math and science camp each summer, where I learned python, chemistry, physics, and a few different kinds of math. The latter sent me to a "special" school for half the day, where I took advanced math and science classes.

In 10th grade, I switched from the Macomb Academy to the St. Clair County Academy, taking classes at St. Clair County Community College instead. I took advanced calculus and chemistry classes with a cohort of students from across the county. I didn't do very well in these classes. I remember being in 11th grade and looking at my report card. All I could see were the Cs that were there, not the fact that I was taking advanced organic chemistry and calc 3 at age 15.

Tenth grade was also the year I found myself a finalist at the International Science and Engineering Fair hosted by Intel in San Jose, California. I made it to ISEF with a project on the physics of tennis, exploring whether the angle of impact plays into whether or not you can ace a ball or score higher. ISEF was a fascinating experience: surrounded by young scientists from all over the globe, having conversations with Nobel Peace Prize winners, and learning more about science and tech than I ever thought possible.

I ended up opting out of the advanced studies program in 12th grade and took classes back at the high school for the full day. I also was finally able to take some more creative classes, like art and varsity choir.

I learned to straddle art and science perfectly, finding that balance between technical and beautiful. Interestingly, all of my corporate-world jobs have been in tech or manufacturing (very scientific jobs) and all of the elements of my creative career have been well...creative. Even the branding on my website proclaims me as the love child of corporate and rock and roll. The reality is, I didn't need to be taking all of those math and science classes. Science was never in the cards as far as a career goes. But taking them set me up to be able to not just attend a liberal arts college, but also to have a truly "liberal arts" career.

I've worked primarily in marketing, though, for companies in differing industries. My grasp on math and science, however limited, helped me understand conversations about ball-bearing weight ratios when I worked at Whirlpool, the complex math that goes into shipping and logistics during my brief time at the distributing company, and even understanding some of the complicated conversions that go into advertiser ROI and automated bidding today at Google. It's served me well as I converse with advertisers and clients in many different industries, and even been helpful in my personal relationships: The last three people I've dated long-term have had highly technical math/science jobs.

> *how can being open to knowledge you wouldn't normally consume help you grow your business or impact your personal life?*

the loss of a mother

LEARNING TO TRUST

The Loss of a Mother

Seven years ago to the day from when this book was published, my mother locked the front door and turned me away, forever.

March 11, 2011, was a snow day. A very cold day. It also was the hottest day on record as far as the tension between my birth mother and me. We'd been struggling to get along for years—in and out of counseling, locked in this ever-present fight about who was right. Only, this wasn't a matter of "Should a child obey her parents?" It was a question of "What do you do when your parent is making fundamentally questionable choices?"

The picture my mother painted of her childhood wasn't pretty. She told a story of growing up in a trailer, of never being the cool kid, and of redefining what it meant to be working class. I was never really clear on just how many stepdads she had; the story was told as though it was a revolving door of men. We kids would joke that we were on our eighth step-grandpa, but the reality is I only ever met two of my grandma's husbands.

The picture my mother painted of her relationship with her own mother was even worse. They never seemed to agree; things were always broken or loud or terrible. When my grandma died (sometime when I was in middle school), my mother wasn't even told about it right away. The story we kids heard was that the will was written such that she wasn't to be told until her mother was in the ground, dead and buried.

As you can imagine, this wasn't the best role model for the kind of parent my mother would become. In some ways, I would argue that she tried hard to be the complete opposite of her mother. But the reality is that in many ways, she ended up much the same.

One Honest Woman

My childhood at first was an idyllic existence. I spent many days after school at Granny and Grampy's house, took piano lessons, had amazing friends, and was generally happy. But the older I grew, the more tense things became.

It was as if my mother's desire to be "better than" her mother drove her to have trophy children. Rather than raise each of her children in a way that was aligned with their unique passion and skills, her almost-power-hungry approach took over. We quickly became props—talking points on a mental index card she trotted out when she needed to prove her parental prowess. My mother truly never accepted less than perfection from her children: She had to have the smartest, most-involved, top gun, leadership-driven, and accomplished kids.

If we were to stop and take a look at my mother's parenting resume, on paper it looks incredible. I was the youngest person at National Flight Academy to solo an airplane. At the time of my Gold Award, I was one of the youngest girls to have attained that level in the Council. When I made cadet lieutenant in the Civil Air Patrol, I had done so in record time from joining the organization. My sister was a nationally recognized expert firearms marksman. My brother attained his Eagle Scout award younger and more quickly than nearly anyone in the organization ever had. We all were in multiple varsity sports, marching band, varsity choir—any organization that could provide us an award. At 15, I was named the Saint Clair County 4-H and Youth Fair Queen—again, one of the youngest to ever attain that recognition.

From the outside looking in, the Fountain family was incredible. We were well-behaved, accomplished, and kids surely destined to do wonderful things.

The reality on the inside? She was raising four incredibly broken children. I came out to my mother when I was barely a teenager. She created a space during a conversation wherein I was led to believe it was safe to share whatever was on my mind, and so I told her. From that day on, it was no longer safe to share my secrets with her.

Her first course of action was to force me to find a boyfriend (and when I failed to do so, she selected one for me). She then encouraged the boy to court me, woo me, and, of course, all the things that come after you start dating. I soon found myself in a relationship with a boy who was encouraged to be physically intimate with me, whether it was touching or kissing, yet I had explicitly made it clear that I was not interested in dating the male gender. My #metoo moments? The first came indirectly from the hands of my mother.

As I continued to "secretly" date women on the side (although nothing was ever secret with my mother), things continued to worsen. Forcing heterosexual relationships transitioned to outright abuse. I once was "sentenced" to more than 1,000 pushups because I was asked to go feed our rabbits but couldn't because I was, literally, physically ill. It was not uncommon in our household to receive lashings with a pistol belt for trivial things like asking to do chores the next day because it was already 10:30 p.m. by the time we got home from our activities.

In fact, the pistol belt came out so frequently that there was one morning in middle school that I arrived at school wearing a bulky hoodie, because I'd caught the belt on my arms to protect my butt. At some point during the day, one of my friends tugged up the sleeves and saw the marks on my arms. She begged me to come home from school with her, and I did. I didn't realize that her dad was a lawyer, and that day a Child Protective Services case was opened.

Back to March 2011. It was my senior year of high school, and tensions with my mother were at an all-time high. I'd had enough. There had been more than one instance of boys touching me inappropriately at my mother's encouragement by that point, not to mention the continued pressures of being out until 10:30 p.m. at activities, needing to come home and do homework, and being up again at 5 a.m. to do farm chores and head to morning swim practice. I was at my breaking point.

That morning, she locked me outside after we'd gotten into an argument. I'd just come off of six months of being grounded for something incredibly trivial, so rather than push the argument further, I opted to go outside and take a lap around the house to cool down. Rather than wait for me to come back inside so we could have a discussion, she locked me outside (no coat, just a t-shirt and pants, on a snow day in Michigan).

When she locked me out, I broke. Something in me finally found the courage to stand up for myself. For some reason, by some stroke of luck, the key to the side door was in the pocket of my sweatpants. I unlocked the door, went up to my room as quietly as I could, and started packing a single bag. I didn't choose to take clothes; I took the notes that my then-girlfriend had written me and my textbooks for school. She figured out I'd gotten back inside and came upstairs. I tried to calmly leave the room, but she physically blocked me inside, pushing me back multiple times. I half-fell back against a dresser, knocking the wind out of me.

Somehow, I was able to get around her, and I walked downstairs and to the front door. During the scuffle, she'd taken my "emergency cell phone" from me, so when I walked outside, I was on my own. I walked down the quarter-mile driveway and turned left on our road, with the intention of walking into town. I planned to make it to the library, call a family friend, and stay with them for the weekend, until my mom and I had both cooled down enough to talk.

I hadn't made it even a mile from the house when a friend drove by. He stopped his Jeep and picked me up. I was grateful, because by that point my sweatpants and Converse were soaked from the snow. He drove me to the library, one hand holding mine while I sobbed in the passenger seat.

When I got to the library, it was really clear that the librarians had no idea what to do with me, but they let me use the phone. I had one phone number memorized: Cyndi, the family friend's (the only phone number I have memorized to this day). I called and briefly explained what had happened. No questions asked, she came and picked me up shortly thereafter. I made it clear to her that I thought I'd only need to stay the weekend—that things would be fine by Monday.

I asked her if we could stop at the bank so I could get some money. I had been working at McDonald's, making about $50 a week, and I went in and pulled out every cent I had (about $175).

One Honest Woman

She was already on her way to her son's band concert, so I went along for the ride. After the concert, it was clear that we needed to get me clothes for the weekend, so she took me to Kmart and I got the cheapest clothes I could find. When we got back to her house, I sent my mother a Facebook message letting her know where I was, that I had no phone, and that I was going to cool off for the weekend.

By Monday morning, my mother and I still hadn't talked, so Cyndi dropped me off at school. I think we both thought I'd end up going home that day. Little did we know, my mother had filed a missing person's report, knowingly defrauding the police, as she knew exactly where I was. I ended up going home with Cyndi, and it was becoming increasingly clear that I was going to be staying with her for a while.

The next few weeks were a blur of change in both my life and in Cyndi's. Two days later, police officers showed up at my Bible Study, apparently still on the hunt for me from the missing person's report. They listened as I explained what had happened and they chose to let me stay. Soon thereafter, Cyndi filed for temporary guardianship over me, as I was living with her and needed medical care and so forth.

Weeks turned to months, and it was increasingly clear that I was never going home. Temporary guardianship was granted, and Cyndi eventually filed for full custody of me. That court hearing was a sobering experience for me: I hadn't spoken to my mother in months, yet there she sat, sobbing as though I was the center of her universe and all she wanted was for me to be safely back in her home.

The judge quickly caught on throughout the proceedings, calling my mother out on her lack of involvement. By the time the case hit his desk, I'd already graduated high school and been in college for three months. Cyndi was the one who threw my high school graduation party. Cyndi was the one who was there as I walked across the stage. Cyndi was the one who moved me into college at the start of the fall semester and kept checking in to make sure I was getting good grades. She'd driven me back and forth to McDonald's all summer so I could continue to work and earn money. She'd paid for my supplies to go to

One Honest Woman

college (sheets for my bed, notebooks, dorm room decor).

My mother hadn't been involved in any of that, nor had she tried to be. Not only had she not been involved, but she'd also actively denied me contact to my three blood siblings. The hearing didn't last long, and, by the end of it, the judge had terminated my mother's parental rights and named Cyndi sole guardian of me. As he banged his gavel, I realized the irony. I was mere days from my 18th birthday.

I thought that that would be the end of the drama and I could begin to live a normal college life, but that wasn't the case. During spring semester of my freshman year, my mother pressed misdemeanor harassment charges against me for trying to remain in contact with my siblings. She actively sought out information on what I was doing at college from one of the professors on campus whom she happened to know.

Yet two years later, in spring 2014, when I was to graduate from the same college, she chose not to attend. I had sent a graduation invite and two tickets to commencement and received no response.

From the moment she took me in, Cyndi became more of a mother to me than my own had ever been. She actively engaged in conversations with me about the choices I was making, gave me unbiased advice even when she didn't agree with my choices, and always supported me, no matter how hard things were. In the six months that I lived with her (and her family) before heading off to college, I experienced for the first time what it was truly like to be a teenager.

Today, seven years later, the woman I call my mom is Cyndi. The family I go home to for holidays is Cyndi's. The family that attended my graduation, celebrated as I started my first job, stood by me through breakups, and cheer me on today as I finish this book is Cyndi's. Her children are my siblings, through and through. What I lost that cold day I left, I've gained back in leaps and bounds.

Growing up, my mother always stressed that "blood is all you'll ever have." When things get bad, we could turn to our blood relatives and they'd be there, no matter what. My childhood taught me that family is what we make of it and that nothing—not even blood—runs stronger than love.

As I stand here seven years later, I can't help but smile. I am the luckiest girl on the planet. I have the most wonderful family and the most incredible friends, and I feel more loved than I ever have.

Readers, indulge me one more time. Should my birth mother ever happen upon this book and read it cover to cover, I hope that she'll see the following:

Lisa,

As I look back on the childhood I had, I cannot help but shudder at what I experienced. I've not spilled that out on these pages; readers have gained more than enough context from what is here. But you and I? We know what happened— the full story.

I stand here, seven years later, and for the first time in my life, I can truly say I do not need you. I no longer belong to you. You can no longer claim ownership of what I have achieved, because the truth is you bear no responsibility for it.

For too long, you've hovered over my life, this silent influence. I no longer have to fight to please you, to be what you deem worthy, because the truth of the matter is that today, you are nobody in my life. A ghost of my past. And today, with one deep inhale and an even deeper exhale, I blow the light in that ghost out and watch as the embers fade to blackness.

I am enough.

heart on
a sleeve

LEARNING TO TRUST

Heart on a Sleeve

It only seems right to start this chapter where the previous one ends: knowing that I am enough. As of this writing, I have 18 tattoos, some big, some small. But the first tattoo, the one that sparked this body art adventure, is a reminder I needed.

Let it be. My first tattoo, three simple words, on the inside of my left wrist. I never planned to get a tattoo and survived the first half of my 18th year on this earth without getting one. But on my 18½ birthday, as one does, I decided it was time. Almost all of my tattoos have dual meanings and it's all thanks to this tattoo. I am of partial British descent, so "let it be" at face value pays homage to the tremendously talented Beatles and their famous song. But deeper than that, this tattoo was a reminder to let what happens, happen when it comes to my relationship with my birth mother.

Ice will suffice. My best friend and I are like fire and ice—complete opposites. We both love the Robert Frost poem as well. She wrote "ice will suffice" on a paper for me, combining two lines of that poem, and on September 15, 2012, I got it tattooed on my right collarbone. At face value, it's a nod to the poem, but deeper than that, it's a reminder that sometimes I need to learn to harden my heart.

Taste of desire. Same poem, different line. I got this tattooed right above the other line three months later, as a reminder that patience is sometimes a good thing.

Where there's Hate, there is Hope. This tattoo, imperfect grammar and all, became my fourth tattoo a week after my third. I'd recently gone rounds with my birth mother, and this was my attempt to remind myself that hope can sometimes spring from hate.

One Honest Woman

Imperfection is beauty, madness is genius. My first tattoo without a deep meaning, this quote was inked on my left collarbone in January 2013. It was meant to be a reminder of all the little stories that make me imperfect but yet feed my larger story so well. This curly hair of mine is one of those stories. My hair sits nestled between *lovely* and *unruly.* If I'm patient, it can be beautiful and straight. If I'm not, it's bouncy and full and very curly—sometimes tightly wound, other times loose like barrel curls. I can't help but smile when I think about participating in the Burgundy Fox photo shoots because it's the *first* time I was ever asked how I wanted to wear my hair for a photo. Most people assume "Oh, she's a white girl. Let's do the long and straight look." But y'all, my hair has BOUNCE. The BF gals let that curl fly free.

Kiss the girl. Ever a *Little Mermaid* fan, this tattoo came next, a secretly punny joke. Of course I love Ariel, but I also kiss girls.

Tomorrow never came. I lost too many friends to too many accidents during my childhood, and a year after Jake Jahn passed away, I got this tattoo on my forearm.

Fate loves the fearless. I finally gave in on my "multiples of three" rule and got this tattoo on my forearm as well. A gentle reminder that we lose 100% of the chances we don't take.

Anchor and cross. My second meaningless tattoo. While dating someone in college, we got tattoos. We didn't get the same tattoo and the meanings of our tattoos weren't intertwined, but I opted for an anchor bisecting a cross.

The world. After a little more than a year in between tattoos, in October 2014 I went back and started on my biggest tattoo to date: a world map taking up my entire left forearm. The map represents my love of travel and, while it's done to current cartographic standards, the style is very "old world."

Ad astra. I studied abroad in Paris in college and have been back a few times since, so for my next tattoo I got the Eiffel Tower with the words *ad astra* next to it. *Ad astra* is Latin for "to the stars." The Eiffel Tower lights up at night with twinkling lights that look like stars.

Red lips. On the same day that I got the ad astra

tattoo, I had red lip prints added to the "kiss the girl" tattoo, just for fun.

The Little Mermaid. My next big project was a little mermaid scene taking up my full right forearm. The scene includes a quote from my favorite *The Little Mermaid* song that reads "the human world, it's a mess" because this tattoo was acquired near the time of all the major terrorist attacks in late 2014 and early 2015.

After that tattoo, I took a nearly two-year break, until summer 2016, when I added two new tattoos.

Aeronautical sectional. The "map" on the back of my right calf is an aeronautical chart of my first solo flight and my first round trip flight as pilot. The map highlights the Lincoln and Omaha, Nebraska, airports, as I learned to fly at Camp Ashland in Nebraska.

Be at peace, not in pieces. On the same day, I got a tattoo in Arabic that loosely translates to "be at peace, not in pieces." At the time, I was halfway through my year of terrorist attack near-misses, and I thought the tattoo an appropriate homage to all that I'd experienced.

Resfeber. In February 2017, I got my two most recent tattoos. The first is the hieroglyph for "explore" with the word *resfeber* under it. *Resfeber* is a Swedish word meaning "the restless race of the traveler's heart before the journey begins, when anxiety and anticipation are tangled together; a travel fever that can manifest as an illness." Since this tattoo wouldn't be seen most days, I also got a smaller version of the glyph on my left wrist bone so I could see it more often.

Tattoos went from something I never planned to do to a way that I commemorate some of the most monumental experiences of my life. Nearly every big moment can be traced back to one of these tattoos and vice versa. I doubt I'll stop at 18, but for now, I'm happy.

a childhood of loss

LIFE'S LITTLE LESSONS

A Childhood of Loss

Saint Clair High School was the place to be if you lived in my county. Some of the best test scores, excellent opportunities, decently ranked sports teams across the board. Our theater program was top notch and our choir program made every budding musician's heart soar. Still today, SCHS is ranked in the top 10% of all of Michigan's high schools, with a graduation rate of 97% and an average ACT that's higher than the state average by 7 points.

However, SCHS was also the best place to be if you wanted to experience loss. From the time I entered ninth grade to the time I completed 12th, the Saint Clair County community lost nearly 100 individuals under the age of 50, higher than the state average by quite a bit. During those four years (and shortly thereafter), I attended far too many funerals of close friends lost to suicide, recklessness, homicide, and other unspeakable causes. By the time I finished college undergrad, more than 10 of my classmates had died.

Carl M. Kruckenberg died November 10, 2009, age 16.
Jake Jahn died March 19, 2012, age 17.
Savannah Blewett died August 18, 2012, age 18.
Erin Elizabeth Stone died September 4, 2015, age 17.
Martin Matthew Hurner died February 6, 2015, age 24.
Roy James "R.J." King IV died October 20, 2014, age 19.
Marcellous "Cells" Redmond died April 12, 2010, age 22.
Sean Parsons and Andrew Davis died November 15, 2009, both age 14.
Kailey Grace Langell died February 11, 2011, age 15.

What does a community do when so many of its young members die at such an early age? How does it impact a person to lose friends before you've even been able to toast to their success?

Little did I know, this experience would go on to prepare me for one of the most shell-shocked years of my young adult life. In about a year's time from November 2015 to November 2016, I narrowly missed four terrorist attacks.

In **November–December 2015**, I went on a trip to Barcelona, Spain. My flights took me through Paris, a happy accident that allowed me a few moments to catch up with my favorite city. However, this was also the same time period of the bombings in Paris (just a few months after the *Charlie Hebdo* shooting).

The attacks were a series of coordinated terrorist events that occurred in Paris, France, and the city's northern suburb of Saint-Denis. Three suicide bombers struck outside the Stade de France in Saint-Denis during a football match. This was followed by several mass shootings and a suicide bombing, at cafés and restaurants. Gunmen carried out another mass shooting and took hostages at an Eagles of Death Metal concert in the Bataclan theater, leading to a stand-off with police. The attackers were shot or blew themselves up when police raided the theater. The attackers killed 130 people, including 89 at the Bataclan. Another 413 people were injured, almost 100 seriously. Seven of the attackers also died, while the authorities continued to search for accomplices. The attacks were the deadliest on France since the Second World War, and the deadliest in the European Union since the Madrid train bombings in 2004. The Islamic State of Iraq and the Levant (ISIL) claimed responsibility for the attacks, saying that it was retaliation for the French airstrikes on ISIL targets in Syria and Iraq. The president of France, François Hollande, said the attacks were an act of war by ISIL. The attacks were planned in Syria and organized by a terrorist cell based in Belgium. In response to the attacks, a three-month state of emergency was declared across the country to help fight terrorism.

In **March 2016**, I was planning to take a trip to Budapest on my own. I'd found an amazing deal on flights and an AirBnb, so I booked it and got excited! However, the day I was supposed to fly out was the day of the terrorist attack on the airport.

The attack was a series of three coordinated suicide bombings, two at Brussels Airport in Zaventem and one at Maalbeek metro station in central Brussels. Thirty-two civilians and three perpetrators were killed, and more than 300 people were injured. Another bomb was found during a search of the airport. The Islamic State of Iraq and the Levant (ISIL) claimed responsibility for the attacks and the perpetrators belonged to a terrorist cell that had been involved in the November 2015 Paris attacks. The Brussels bombings happened shortly after a series of police raids targeting the group. The bombings were the deadliest act of terrorism in Belgium's history.

In **June 2016**, I took a trip to Thailand. Due to a delay on my flight from Chicago to Rome, my travel route changed and I had to fly through Istanbul, Turkey. Istanbul was home to a terrorist attack that same month.

The attack consisted of shootings and suicide bombings at Atatürk Airport in Istanbul. Gunmen armed with automatic weapons and explosive belts staged a simultaneous attack at the international terminal. Forty-five people were killed, in addition to the three attackers, and more than 230 people were injured. Monitoring group Turkey Blocks identified widespread internet restrictions affecting the entire country in the aftermath of the attack. Turkish officials said the attackers were acting on behalf of the Islamic State of Iraq and Levant (ISIL) and had come to Turkey from ISIL-controlled Syria. No one publicly claimed responsibility for the attack.

After all this, one might imagine that I would be averse to traveling. However, it failed to hamper my passion for travel, and in **August 2017** I found myself in the aftermath of yet another attack.

On the 17th of August 2017, a young man drove a van into pedestrians on La Rambla in Barcelona, Spain, killing 13 people and injuring at least 130 others, one of whom died 10 days later, on August 27th. Nine hours after the Barcelona attack, five men thought to be members of the same terrorist cell drove into pedestrians in nearby Cambrils, killing one woman and injuring six others. All five attackers were shot and killed by police. The night before the Barcelona attack, an explosion occurred in a house in the Spanish town of Alcanar, destroying the building and killing two members of the terrorist cell, including the 40-year-old imam thought to be the mastermind. Amaq News Agency attributed indirect responsibility for the attack to the Islamic State of Iraq and the Levant (ISIL).

The perpetrators of the attack were of Moroccan descent. I had arrived in Morocco on August 16th, and throughout my stay a manhunt was on for a few of the perpetrators. My time in Casablanca was pleasant, though full of military police, unannounced spot checks for identification, and roadblocks in places that were usually open to the public.

I've never been someone who's been particularly afraid during travel, but this time period gave me some pause. Friends joked that they were going to check with me before they went anywhere because I was a magnet for terrorists, but honestly it was frightening!

I still travel without hesitation today, but I've learned that you can't always be certain that things will be safe, no matter where you're going. This accidental dose of humanity has found its way into other areas of my life, reminding me to take the risk, because it's not worth it to be afraid.

> *the unpredictability of life is one of its core joys and greatest sorrows—the moments that happen seemingly by accident end up having the greatest impact. what are your accidentally life-changing experiences?*

agitating and tumbling

GROWING UP

Agitating and Tumbling

When I was in undergrad, I interviewed for a job at Whirlpool Corporation (the appliance company). I was fortunate enough to get hired in November of my senior year and was able to spend the rest of my senior year not worrying, knowing I had a job starting that following summer.

Whirlpool structures new hires into a variety of different leadership development programs, or LDPs. I was hired into the brand management LDP and started on July 7, 2014.

Whirlpool was an interesting job to have right out of college—and one of the most challenging experiences of my career. I was working at a $20B company at 20 years old, collaborating with world-class advertising agencies, and talking to product managers with 40 years of experience on a daily basis. That's equal parts a really inspiring opportunity (to be trusted with so much right out of the gate) but also really scary (it's *a lot* of responsibility).

At right about my 30th day working at Whirlpool, my boss left the company. She was offered an absolutely incredible opportunity that she couldn't pass up, and I didn't begrudge her exit. A new person filled that role, but the dynamic of the team had definitely changed. Whirlpool's structure is such that the ratio of manager to reports is rarely more than three or four people per manager (whereas Google is closer to 11 to 13 per manager). In my specific case, I was my manager's only direct report. New employee, brand new manager. Recipe for disaster, considering we were just weeks away from the biggest rebrand the company had ever experienced.

It ended up being one of the single best experiences of my career.

There are two things I know about myself

inherently: I have a passion for time lines, and I do best when I have a clear direction. Time lines and direction were nonexistent in this situation, due to all the newness circling around.

I quickly had the opportunity to take on some *massive* projects as a result of the chaos. I got to manage millions of dollars in marketing spend, spent more than a few days on set supervising a commercial shoot, helped with fulfillment logistics for a giveaway on *The Ellen Show*, and was able to collaborate with people I might not have normally had exposure to.

Perhaps the most exciting project I had was getting to help ideate the strategy for the commercialization of a new consumer packaged good (CPG) for Whirlpool Laundry. The project meant meetings in Chicago, talking with many different teams inside Whirlpool, and finally getting to see the project take shape at the Consumer Electronics Show in 2015.

All this responsibility for someone my age and at my level of experience was intimidating, but there was honor to be found in the grit of grinding it out and learning how to thrive in that environment. Many of the skills I learned at Whirlpool have served me incredibly well in my roles since. I've often thought about how differently my life would have turned out if Whirlpool hadn't been the start to my post-grad career.

> *having a corporate career at 20 meant being the intentional outcast: too young, too inexperienced, unable to drink. what moments when you've felt left out have turned out to have a lasting impact?*

thrice fired

DISAPPOINTING MOMENTS

Thrice Fired

I still remember the day like it was yesterday. I was having a conversation with a friend's dad, who was running for State Senate at the time (he was a sitting State Representative), and he was telling me about everything he was working on. I knew we had differing opinions on politics but, at the time, I thought I was going to major in pre-law when I left for college the following year, so when he asked me if I'd like to help work on his campaign I said yes. I quickly became youth campaign manager, creating and executing strategies for how to reach the younger voters in his constituency (even though I wasn't yet of voting age). He went on to win that Senate seat, and I returned to high school to complete my senior year. Over the next four years, as I finished high school and college, he went on to win re-election, and I even did an internship in his office to satisfy my college internship requirements.

Life, however, isn't always sunflowers and roses. During that same time period, I was fired from a job. During my middle year of college, I got a job working as a marketing associate for a mold release manufacturer. Mold release is a chemical agent that aids in releasing molded industrial parts from their dies on a manufacturing line and is comprised of very intense, very hard-to-market chemicals. In the manufacturing world, this product was as necessary and unsexy as toilet paper: Everyone needed it, and nobody cared where it came from—just that it worked. Competing on price was inevitable, and this became my first lesson in the importance of differentiation.

Soon after starting at the company, the CEO called me into his office and we started talking about stretch goals. He asked me about my dreams and where I wanted to go in life, and I revealed that I wanted to be a full-time entrepreneur (a goal I didn't know I had until talking him through my future). We both were surprised at this revelation, as I'd applied for the job stating a desire to diversify my experience before going to law school at Dartmouth College, and had been hired under the assumption that I'd build a career there that would take me through undergrad and maybe even a few years after. He told me the story of starting his company—the one where I was working—and how, in 20 years time, he grew it from a fledgling research company to the multi-million-dollar entity it had become. He invited me to craft a business proposal for what my own entrepreneurial pursuit would look like, indicating he'd review it and provide his thoughts.

I did just that, working night and day over a three-day weekend to produce an impressive 15-page business plan, complete with a logo (my first attempt at graphic design), a full market survey, and clear plans on how I, too, was going to grow my business to a multi-million-dollar entity. On Monday morning, I left it on his desk with a note that thanked him for his time and invited every ounce of critique he had. I also sent it via email in a Word doc in case he wanted to make notes using "track changes." He never reviewed that document, and a few days later, when the office manager asked me if I'd take out the trash, I found it in the top of his office waste basket, note unopened.

Not long after this conversation, it became clear that our paths were diverging. At his initial encouragement, I'd started spending my nights building a website on Wordpress and seeking clients. During the day, I was helping the company put together its final year of attendance at a trade show as we all struggled to identify our key differentiator; it was obvious the upward trajectory of the company was starting to falter. On a Friday morning, I was called into the HR director's office, where I was informed that I was being let go. The company had decided to go a different direction. Dejected, I left the office that day wondering if this unintentional entrepreneurial dream had cost me the job and vowed to set that dream aside to refocus on the always-alluring Dartmouth Dream.

Fast-forward two years and I found myself in a similar situation. I'd graduated from undergrad and was nearly finished with my master's. I'd spent an incredible year working for Whirlpool

One Honest Woman

Corporation absorbing everything I could ever want to know about manufacturing and large-scale marketing. I'd had the opportunity to work on one of the biggest rebrand projects that the advertising world had ever seen, and I was completely obsessed with the experience. At the behest of a budding romance, I moved to Chicago and took a new job, this time with a wholesale distributor.

Wholesale distribution is eerily similar to mold release agents: Every hospital and restaurant needs toilet paper and soap, and they really don't care where it comes from, as long as it's cheap. The running joke in the office was that nothing could ever be an emergency, because we weren't saving the world, we were just selling toilet paper. Soon after I started, the CMO invited me to attend a Chicago Cubs game with the marketing team, and we had a conversation about dreams and goals. Remembering the softened pain of my last experience on this topic, I avoided entrepreneurship and instead talked about my love of travel. He recommended the name of an airport driver, and we swapped war stories about harrowing experiences we'd had abroad.

Soon thereafter, an opportunity arose. I was invited to go to New York City to attend an entrepreneurial event at no cost to me. I'd put the "entrepreneurial thing" on the back burner, but my travel-loving heart couldn't bear to pass up a free trip to NYC. Since I was new to the company, I didn't have any vacation time with which to attend the event, so I decided to write a proposal identifying all the things I'd be able to bring back to the company after attending the event. I even offered to work 12-hour days the week preceding the event to make up for the time I'd be off work. My manager softly indicated that if it was her, she wouldn't go. She felt the experience was a scam and that I'd get hurt. The vice president of HR agreed to let me go, as long as I made up all the hours I missed by working those 12-hour days. Grateful for the opportunity, I flew to New York ready to absorb everything I could.

When I came back just 72 hours later, notebook and ideas in hand, things had changed at work. A few of my key projects had been offloaded to an intern, and my manager seemed cold. I scheduled a 1:1 to discuss the event, share my learnings, and seek ways to bridge the gap, but I left that 1:1 just as dejected as when I'd arrived. Her soft hint at a scam was actually a silent desire for me not to attend the event at all, because she didn't want me out of the office.

A few more months went by, our relationship seemingly rebuilt, and I finally had vacation time to spend. After working hard to put together our company's attendance at nearly 20 trade shows in seven weeks, I was excited to take a few days off and go to Budapest. After wrapping up all of my work neatly, I asked if there was anything else I could do before I left. My manager simply smiled and told me to have a great time.

Budapest was a whirlwind and I came back reenergized. After seeing a city that sat in WWII ruins nearly 60 years after the war ended, I was inspired to re-infuse some energy into the distribution company. I approached my manager with ideas and the equivalent of $10 in Hungarian Forints, my token souvenir to her from the trip. She smiled and asked me to schedule a meeting to discuss the ideas. I headed back to my desk and fired off a calendar invite with a brief outline of all that had inspired me.

Shortly after lunch that day, I was called into the CMO's office. My commitment to the company was called into question due to my passion for travel. My manager informed me that when I'd worked those 12-hour days to make up for being out of town, company policy dictated that she had to be at the office, too (although she'd never mentioned that when I accepted the trip six months prior) and she'd felt inconvenienced by my desire to jettison across the globe. I was told that my position was being eliminated since an intern was handling most of my workload anyway *(ah, so that's why my key projects had been offloaded)*, and I was asked to pack my things and leave immediately.

I left that day feeling angry. Again I'd been asked to share my dreams, and again those dreams had been the eventual cause of my exit from the company. I decided to recommit to my entrepreneurial dreams. I invested big time, setting myself up for success, and I had the spring of a lifetime. However, all dreams come with equally big fears. Near the end of June, I found myself feeling scared. I sought another corporate job and was quickly hired at a local steel manufacturer, a subsidiary of a very large conglomerate of companies. I was to report directly to the director of sales and was told that I had free reign to reinvigorate sales in a dying company in a dying industry. I was excited by the challenge!

The company was to participate in the biggest manufacturing trade show on the planet just 60 days after I started, and it was my responsibility to learn the industry and find a way for us to make a splash at this show. (Are you starting to see a trend? Manufacturing companies. Trade shows. Big expectations.) I was up for the challenge and dived in, learning about shim stock, metal hardnesses, the difference between O1 and W1 drill rod, and many other elements of the industry. I even learned to take sales calls, report transactions in a program reminiscent of MS-DOS, and how to package cut shim.

We put together an event for the trade show booth that we thought would draw in visitors in hordes: the shim challenge. Shim stock is often cut by hand by machinists working in manufacturing facilities. The thinner the shim, the more likely it is to tear or be inaccurately made. Our company had a product that allowed for the inside and outside diameter of lengthening/shortening shim to be made with complete precision and in less than 10% of the time of manual production. The show went off without a hitch, and we gained about five new accounts from the event—a big deal for any company, but an even bigger deal for this dying company.

A couple weeks after the trade show, I left town to attend an entrepreneurial conference. When I was hired, before I even signed the dotted line, I'd requested permission to attend the conference, so I assumed there would be no issue at all with my attendance. I learned so much and when I came back, the director of sales asked me if there had been any lessons at the conference that applied to both "Dannie International" (his half-joking name for my still-budding LLC) and the company I worked for. I shared everything that I thought applied to both places, and he seemed pleased with the results, taking notes throughout our conversation.

About a week later, it was time for my 90-day review. I hadn't had a formal review with my supervisor until this point, and he called me into his office along with the sales manager to discuss everything I'd worked on. They were incredibly pleased with the results of the trade show and even more pleased with the website I'd begun redesigning for them, but I could tell something was off. After about a half hour of conversation, the truth was revealed: The big conglomerate couldn't justify having me employed at the dying steel company anymore. I'd served my purpose in putting together a plan for the show, but they didn't foresee enough work for me over the next eight months until the next show to justify keeping me employed. Once again, and for the second time in six months, I was let go.

I left feeling dejected and angry, frustrated that I hadn't trusted my entrepreneurial endeavours enough and knowing that I was now three months further behind for seemingly no reason at all. A couple days later, I left for Inspired Retreat, where I finally decided to lean into being an entrepreneur—three years to the day after getting fired from that first job.

Fast-forward to today: That first company has since gone out of business. The second company lost its foothold as market leader in a dying industry and is fighting to regain its place. The third company reported lower sales in 2016 than it's reported in nearly 10 years. Me? I've finally leaned in to trust my entrepreneurial pursuits and I'm doing just fine.

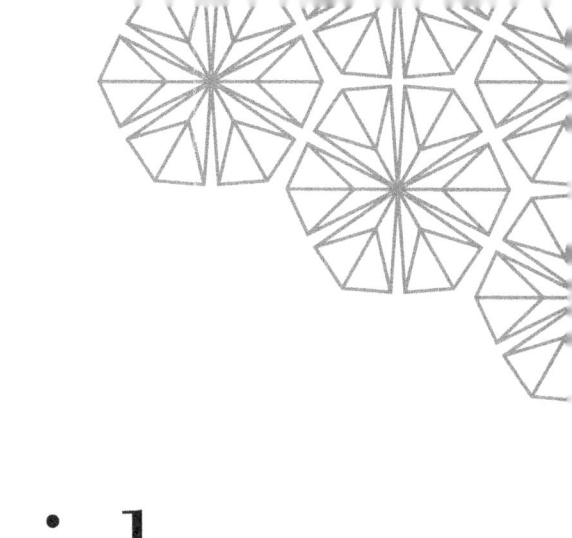

girls, girls, girls

LEARNING TO LOVE

Girls, Girls, Girls

Anyone who knows me just a little knows that I wear my heart on my sleeve. It's perhaps my greatest downfall in life. It should come as no surprise, then, that I've loved hard and had my heart broken more than once.

My first love was the kind that they write YA romance novels about. It burned slow, for years, and then promptly set on fire and went up in flames. The first time we met, I was in second grade. She was in third. She seemed like the most awesome of little girls, and I instantly wanted to be her friend.

Seven years later, a few weeks before I started

my freshman year of high school, we were in a summer program together G-chatting side by side. By this time, we were truly the best kind of inseparable friends. She finished my sentences; I started hers. Was this flirting? What's happening! Why is my heart so heavy, my hands so numb? During lunch break we both went downstairs and that's when it happened: She kissed me. It was electric. There I was, 13 years old, kissing a *girl*. I stood there, frozen, and she kissed me again. She whispered softly that there was nothing to be afraid of and then I kissed her back. We never actually said the words, but as of that moment, we were together.

Our romance was the classic "early aughts" tale. Growing up in a midwestern small town meant that there weren't any other lesbians at high school—at least, none who were out. We had no idea what we were doing; all we knew was that it was fun. We had different lunch periods, but every day I'd meet her at her locker before fourth period with a note I'd written over lunch. Folded into a perfect square, it fit perfectly in her front pocket, and she'd read it as we walked to class—always smiling. Between fifth and sixth periods, she'd meet me at my locker and slip a note in my back pocket. This was dating. ***It was bliss.***

We ended up breaking up as she headed into her senior year and she started dating a sophomore named Stefany. Stefany was a cheerleader and I was jealous. Stefany became my first and only high school fistfight. She punched me, and I punched her back. She got a five-day suspension.

The relationship itself seemed to go smoothly, but the mechanics of what was going on behind the scenes would become our eventual demise.

My birth mother (unsurprisingly) was anti-gay. She also was very against this specific girl because she found her to be pretentious and disrespectful. She started bribing my little brother with $5 every time he caught us kissing. The girl and I turned this on its head by intentionally kissing, and then my brother would split his "winnings" with us. However, also unsurprisingly, this also served to further ruin my relationship with her.

A variety of other factors contributed to the

decline of the relationship. Her mother made her break up with me on the phone (although neither the girl or I adhered to this breakup) and the girl signed my yearbook one year simply with the words "I love you" (and no name), which became a source of contention in my house for a while.

Unfortunately, due to my birth mother's desire that I not date a girl, I was also required to take a boy as my date to formal functions. I was taken out on dates by boys as well, even though my birth mom knew I liked this girl.

I had lunch with some friends recently and we were talking about the experiences we had when we were 13 and 14. The majority of us came out of the closet (originally as lesbian) at around 12 or 13. As is often the case, our parents were none too happy with this development, and so we found ourselves practicing ethical non-monogamy.

We were dating one another—girls learning what it's like to date other girls, kiss other girls, love other girls. But at the same time, to please our parents, we had to date boys. We carefully selected our male partners: boys we liked, boys we were friends with, boys who knew what was going on and that we were not exactly straight. And so our non-monogamy began.

At age 16, I was navigating a year-plus relationship (it's questionable how strongly the word *relationship* can be used at this age) with a girl and also a year-plus relationship with a boy. Both knew of the another and very basic polyamorous practices were in place. I had actual date nights with both of them (separately), intimate romantic and sexual relationships with both of them, and feelings of love (or whatever teenage love is called) with both of them.

In fact, when I headed to college just a few months after that, I still practiced non-monogamy, though this time voluntarily. I no longer was connected to my parents, but I still found myself seeing both the woman and the man.

By age 18, I was still in a relationship with the woman (and she'd had other partners beside me, both male and female) and actively dating a new man.

While I don't believe that dating in your teens is quite the accurate comparison to dating as an adult, I do find it fascinating that due to coming out, I found myself practicing polyamory at such a young age and in such an ethical manner. I even managed to take both my boyfriend and my girlfriend to my high school junior prom as my dates without issue.

As my friends and I sat talking about this recently, we all realized how those early experiences shaped our dating as adults. Many of us identify as queer now, rather than lesbian. We also saw the differences between our teenage and adult experiences with polyamory and how, interestingly, our teenage selves felt less emotional stress at the prospect.

I look back on this period of my life with mixed feelings. I'm impressed that I had the emotional intelligence to manage multiple relationships and never leave a partner unsatisfied. I also somehow was able to understand the importance of being open and honest with all parties, even at that age.

However, my heart remains utterly disappointed

One Honest Woman

that I even had to grapple with non-monogamy at such a young age, simply because my mother couldn't respect my preferences when it came to dating. It's fascinating to me: Most parents don't want their children dating at all. Of those who do let their children date, many are *grateful* when their child is gay (in my case, no accidental teenage pregnancies!). But my reality was that my mother not only wanted me to date, it was a mandate that I dated men.

> *how do you handle situations in which what your loved ones want isn't what you want? we face this as entrepreneurs all the time—trying to explain why we'd quit our jobs to run businesses full-time.*

the girl without a home

LEARNING TO TRUST

The Girl Without a Home

In August 2016, in the lobby of an absolutely gorgeous hotel, a quiet girl turned to an impressive coach and said, "I want to be a speaker someday—like all of you."

Less than 30 days later, she walked into her first entrepreneurial speaking gig, in front of just eight women, and brought the metaphorical house down.

Now, she's a formally recognized international speaker, a visible force in the entrepreneurial space, and a woman who finds herself on folks' dream speaker wish lists.

I've always been a travel aficionado, but 2017

redefined what that meant for me.

Prior to 2017, I was *the biggest* designer purse girl. I collected them like candy and had the prettiest set of Kate Spade, Valentino, and Chanel bags, to name a few. I also was a fan of pretty things, of a well-decorated home, and of collecting clutter (unintentionally).

But 2017 was the year of no home. Being on the road doesn't mesh well with fancy handbags or pretty decor, so I set them aside (and actually sold most of them). Setting them aside became more than just a practical move: It became a way for me to ditch the nonsense and live life a little more intentionally.

I started carrying around just a backpack, full of only the most essential work and life items. However, I still wanted a way to show my individuality, and thus my pin collection was born. Rather than valuing my personality through a designer leather good, I showcase the best (and worst!) parts of myself through the enamel pins on my backpack.

Some of my favorites: The thank-you pin from

One Honest Woman

Adam J Kurtz, because I write *every* person who lets me stay in their home a handwritten thank-you note. The I am very busy pin from BanDo, because 64 speaking gigs in one year is INSANE. The #pettybitch pin from The Blank Bitch because I get a little crazy sometimes. And an assortment of pins from Autostraddle because—YAY!—sexuality spectrum.

Real talk, though: Fewer than three feet from that backpack on any given day are a pile of dirty laundry, a messy unmade bed, a girl who hasn't washed her hair in three days, and an overflowing to do list. It's real life around here, always.

When I made the decision to go it alone, I got so many questions: *Why would you give up your apartment? How can you live out of a suitcase? What even prompted the decision?*

Let's take a step back.

In November 2016, I was finally getting started on my PowerSheets around Thanksgiving, when I realized that I was only going to be home six days a month or so throughout 2017. Why would

I pay for an apartment that would, in essence, be a glorified storage unit? I decided the best move would be to downsize my belongings by more than 75% and "go nomad," and so I moved out of my apartment (breaking a two-year lease 18 months early) the day before my birthday and hit the road.

In 2017, I was on the road essentially 24/7. I flew nearly 250,000 miles, drove another 25,000, visited countless cities and countries, and connected with so many entrepreneurial friends I'd only met online previously. The girl who was perhaps the most active user of the "pre-plan" method was now planning places to stay less than 24 hours before. It was all brand new and, frankly, it was scary.

I learned a lot of humility in 2017. It's not that I was necessarily a prideful person before that, but asking for help has never been my strong suit. Perhaps my most striking memory of this comes from June 2017. I had planned to stay at a new hotel opening in Nashville, Tennessee, and do some PR work with them on Instagram. However, they had oversold the rooms and unfortunately couldn't host me. Less than 24 hours prior to my departure for Nashville, I was suddenly going to be homeless. I put out an alert in a couple of entrepreneurial Facebook groups, and in less than an hour, I had a new place to stay. Not just a place to stay, but upon going to tag my hosts on Instagram, I discovered they were the designers on the HGTV show *Masters of Flip.*

2017 was a string of happy accidents like this one.

Day drinking in a bookstore? I spent some time in February in Portland speaking at the Together Experience, getting tattoos, and catching up with business friends. I also took a moment to visit the Multnomah Whiskey Library and Powell's Books.

If you know anything about me, you know that whiskey and books are quite possibly my second-greatest happy place (behind travel, of course). The day that I visited these places, I started off in Powell's rare book room and finished with an incredible taste of whiskey. Both of these locations draw hordes of visitors, but they have very different contents (try drinking at Powell's: I doubt you'll get far). Even though they're only a couple blocks apart, they're both wildly successful, despite their overlapping demographics.

It got me thinking: Even if we cater to the same audience as someone else, we have something different to offer. There are actually studies out there that link a passion for whiskey with a passion for reading. Don't believe me? Consider this: New York City's five boroughs have no less than 12 bars that cater to reading while sipping your favorite beverage (most commonly whiskey). Knowing this, it's safe to assume that visitors to Portland who want to see MWL also want to visit Powell's. Why might someone visit both places? Because they go to MWL to taste rare whiskeys and enjoy the environment that accompanies those beverages, while they go to Powell's to get lost down an aisle of books and smell that comfortable and familiar old book smell. Find your differentiator.

Real-life entrepreneurial money launderer? April was a crazy travel month for me. I spent an overnight in 10 cities and passed through quite a few more on my journey. Logic would follow that April would be the worst month for me to be without money, right? Well, karma just knows how to get you sometimes. Curious? Let me fill you in.

On my first day in Toronto, I got a phone call. I mean, I get a lot of phone calls, but this phone call I actually answered. It was my bank, calling to let me know that all my accounts were frozen, pending review, because of some supposed shady dealings.

Let that sink in for a second: This 23-year-old nomad is apparently a money launderer or some kind of drug runner or something. I was also stranded in a foreign country with just $120 cash to my name until I made it back to the States. The bank was curious: (a) Why did I have so many trips booked to the Middle East in the next year, (b) Why was I in so many countries so near to terrorist attacks, and (c) Why had I been stopped at TSA so much lately? Not sure how my bank knew about all of that (or how that's relevant to my money), but I digress.

Not only that, but it was the beginning of the month. That meant that all the business subscriptions I have (Zoom, ConvertKit, etc.) went unpaid, because my bank declined all those transactions due to the same supposed shady dealings.

Whoops. Here's the thing, though: It doesn't matter what you tell the world you are, the world will form its own opinion. My bank account is formed under a legally registered LLC. There's an EIN number attached. They have my personal details. If you google me (or my business), you'll find pages upon pages of articles, guest blogs I've done, podcast interviews, and even my own content. If my business is a front for money laundering, I've done a really good job at crafting that cover story.

Speed trap? In April, my travels also took me home to see my family for the first time in nearly two years! That trip home was a week of adventuring in my hometown and catching up with old friends. Lots of trips down memory lane—and one particular trip that (might) cost me a chunk of change.

On Saturday night of the week I was home, I was driving to pick up my sister's fiance and take her into town to meet my sister. There's a section of the road that goes from 35 mph to 45 mph to 60 mph in a distance of about 100 yards. I turned onto this road, minding my own business, and headed the five miles down the road to their house. Shortly before arriving, a state trooper pulled me over.

As he walked up to my car and I rolled down my window, he said, "Ma'am, are you aware of why I pulled you over?" I indicated that I wasn't and he explained that five miles prior, at the intersection, he clocked me going 78 mph in the 35 mph zone.

What?! In typical (very respectful) Dannie fashion, I asked if he could tell me what the radar flagged me traveling at. He simply restated that five miles prior, at the intersection, he clocked me going 78 mph in the 35 mph zone. He went back to his car with my license and registration, and returned a short time later with a ticket for 65 in a 55 (a zone not even available on that stretch of road) with a note that said he clocked me going 78 (no indication of which zone). I thanked him for the ticket and continued about my day (though obviously very frustrated by the situation).

Here's the thing: Your metrics and others' metrics often don't match up—and others might be in a position to challenge the validity of your metrics without you having room to do the same.

"Less than" hustle. In May, I officially celebrated two years of Side Hustle Gal acclaim. I also celebrated two years since I "came out of the closet" as a part-time entrepreneur. Before that, I hid it. My clients didn't know I had a full-time job, and my full-time job didn't know I was side hustling. In fact, I don't even think my entrepreneur friends knew I had a full-time job. In the moment that I breathed the words "I'm a Side Hustle Gal," I knew something had to change. I didn't deserve to feel ashamed (and neither did anyone else who was killing it as a SHG).

In that moment (and a few moments after that), the idea for the Side Hustle Gal community was born. I bought a domain and started to let the idea fester. In March 2016 I started writing a book, in summer 2016 I invited friends to join me on that ride, and in fall 2016 *The Side Hustle Gal* was published.

Since then, I've published a second and third book, started a podcast lifting up new and part-time entrepreneurs, gone full-time entrepreneur and back to side hustle again. Here's the thing: *Side hustle* is not a synonym for *less than* hustle. It's just a phrase we use when we choose not to pursue our entrepreneurial business full time, for whatever reason.

2017 was also the year of conferences. Prior to 2017, I'd spoken mostly at smaller events, related to marketing or community organizations I'd been a part of. In late 2016, with the help of a business coach and a speaking coach (Reina Pomeroy and Jessica Rasdall, respectively), I went on a pitching spree. By the end of 2016, I had booked a dozen or so speaking gigs, and by the end of 2017, I had completed more than 60 speaking engagements during my "nomad year."

As someone who was not very visible online at the time of starting this process, I am truly floored by how far we've been able to come in that amount of time. Additionally, many of these conferences invited me to give more than one presentation at the event.

Beyond just speaking gigs, I've also worked with brand partners and through other avenues to complete parallel projects while at the conferences or cities in question.

By the end of 2017, I had slept in nearly 25 Airbnbs, 15 friends' couches, 14 "friend of a friend's" guest rooms, 10 different Kimpton Hotels properties (some more than once), and eight miscellaneous hotels.

I flew approximately 300,000 miles and put about 20,000 miles on my car (a lease—not my smartest move).

I incurred a whopping $52,000 in travel expenses including meals, fuel, flights, places to sleep, and rental cars where necessary (some paid by brands and conferences and some paid out of pocket). Travel is not cheap, even when you're traveling solo like I was.

I discovered amazing places like Voodoo Doughnuts, Glory Hole Doughnuts (sensing a theme?), 4505 BBQ, and more street vendors and food trucks than I could ever count. I lived nearly entirely off street vendors while in Morocco and Portland. I fell in love with Gilt Bar (Chicago), Compass Coffee (DC), Sightglass Coffee (San Francisco), Besaw's (Portland), Rogue Brewhouse (Portland), The Burger's Priest (Toronto), The Works (Toronto), and just about any other place I geotagged on Instagram in 2017. I rediscovered my love of Slow's BBQ, In-n-Out, and Buddy's Pizza.

2017 taught me a lot about travel, too.

Don't try new (or new-to-you) food the night before a speaking engagement. You *will* get food poisoning or an upset stomach; it's just Murphy's law.

Don't always go for the cheapest Airbnb. You might end up sharing a "one-bedroom" loft apartment with five men for 11 days straight.

Just because you're traveling doesn't mean you can't hole up and just watch Netflix for an entire day. Even nomads need a break.

TSA Pre✓ and Global Entry are mandatory (if you get GE, you get TSA Pre✓ included)—no exceptions. So much time is wasted in line for security, and I cannot tell you how many times I nearly missed a flight in 2017.

Always carry cash. Period.

Pack less than you think you'll need, and then cut what you packed in half again. You'll spend most of your days alone and nobody will notice if you wear a pair of pants twice.

Speaking of being alone, nomad life is lonely. Co-work in community spaces and create opportunities for chatter and conversation.

I may have settled back down for 2018 and beyond but many of my nomad lessons have remained: minimalism, backpacks not purses, and learning to plan a little bit less, to name a few.

> *travel creates opportunities for exploration, learning new things, and experiencing what it's like to live a different life. how can you bring these opportunities into your every day, even if you're not traveling?*

i love lamp

LEARNING TO TRUST

I Love Lamp

It's crazy to think that when this book comes out and you hold it in your hands, it will have been going on two years since I was packing up what was to be my last solo apartment. I'd said yes to moving two states over and more than eight hours from home because I'd fallen in love with who I thought was my forever person. We were in the final stages of moving in together. Little did I know that a week later, I'd come home from the most amazing trip overseas to a completely different person—someone who was completely not in love with me and who saw my business and the fire in my heart for entrepreneurship as something that hindered my ability to be human.

The truth is, I didn't come home to a different person. I just came home to someone finally brave enough to tell me she felt differently about things.

Having nearly two years of distance from that experience has made so many things clear to me. As I sit here and reflect on everything that's happened, that breakup was almost a metamorphosis. That life-changing event, no matter how painful, served as the catapult that launched me to where I am today.

I would never have imagined that I'd be where I am today. I had no idea that I could be an international speaker, a sought-after marketing strategist, a podcaster, someone whom people look up to, someone who is respected. At the time, my brand wasn't even my name, the idea of nomad life hadn't even crossed my mind, the concept of charging what I was worth was so foreign to me that my partner was helping me *decrease* the amount of my quotes because she (and by proxy, I) believed that I didn't need to be charging that much.

I was in love with someone who saw my business and the fire in my heart for entrepreneurship

as something that hindered my ability to be human.

Talk about gut-wrenching.

I say all this to tell you that starting over wasn't easy. Separating my identity from hers, finding my true self again; it was all a fight. I made so many bad decisions in that first month after we split. I had allowed my worth to be defined by her approval. It took months for me to redefine my worth as something that I owned, and it's still something that I struggle with today. But it was worth the effort. If you're struggling to see your true self, know that it's okay for you to just begin again, too. Take that first breath, then take the leap.

Back in 2016 when the breakup happened, I had been been doing some serious soul searching. I realized I'd been making decisions for us and for what I thought we wanted, but I wasn't being true to myself. As business owners, we have so many outside pressures weighing on the decisions we have to make on a daily basis that sometimes we forget to be true to who we are. At the end of the day, we are the sole (or co-) owner of our business. We are responsible for the results of our decisions, and we have to make the decisions that make the most sense for us. This was a hard lesson to learn.

After a bit of time, things got easier and I started dating again, thinking I was ready.

The first girl I went on a date with post-breakup was an incredibly talented social worker. We had a great time on our first date, but I definitely put my foot in my mouth. My experience with social workers hasn't been great, due to everything with my mom, and I pre-judged this girl based on that past experience, rather than being open to the fact that she might be different. Naturally, we didn't end up working out (though today she is engaged to be married and seems to be happier than ever!).

My next date was with a talented student. She'd just moved to America from Lebanon, and we had a great time talking about history and a variety of topics. She ended up opting to date a man instead, so we went our separate ways.

After that was an experience that forever

changed my perspective on dating. I went on a date with a comedienne performing in a scripted comedy at Second City. Our dates were great: We had good conversation about a variety of different things and had overlapping histories in many ways. The dates went so well that she ended up inviting me to see her show. The show itself was fantastic, and I would highly recommend it to anyone who's able to see it, but the improv section in the middle left me a little confused. All in all, it felt like our connection had been more about me tagging her on Instagram (and thus leveraging whatever followers I had) versus building a true connection. We got drinks after the show, but for obvious reasons didn't end up seeing each other again.

Shortly thereafter, I met a welder. It was right around Halloween and one of our first dates was going to a haunted house together. I am deathly scared of all things jumpy, loud, or dark, so haunted houses are definitely an adventure for me. We managed to survive that date, but things died out soon thereafter. She was only four years older but was in a very different life place than I was.

As if the last string of dates wasn't enough, the next was perhaps the most complex yet! She was the curator of the data library at a particle physics research lab outside Chicago. We ended up going on dates every single Monday night for about six months, but it became clear that we were more friends than potential romantic partners. She was absolutely brilliant and I walked away from every date with so much to consider (and a bit of a headache).

After that, I made a *big* mistake. I met a girl with the same name as my ex and with many of the same mannerisms as my ex too. (The only major difference was that my ex stood nearly 6 feet tall and this girl was 4'11".) Our first date went well, and we went on a couple more, but it quickly became hot and cold, and I just didn't want to deal with the drama of constantly struggling to figure out where we stood.

During this year of dating, I also experienced my first ghosting. I met a girl shortly after things fizzled out with the 4'11" girl. My friends called this girl Skrillex, because she looked like the female version of the DJ. We hit it off and had amazing chemistry as well as great conversation. Three months into talking, she disappeared for about two weeks. I let it go, assuming she wasn't interested anymore, until she resurfaced with apologies and our conversation picked back up. After about four months of talking back and forth, we started talking about meeting up. She lived six hours away, but I was going to be driving through her city on the way to Nashville, so timing was perfect. I was to text her when I was an hour out and we'd sort things out. I texted an hour out and half an hour out, and she never replied. In fact, she didn't reply for more than a month. Again I assumed I'd been ghosted. Later that fall, I got a Twitter DM blaming me for the ghosting and stating that I broke her heart. I didn't know what to say.

After a year of seemingly endless dead-end dates, things started to clean up. This whole time, I had been on OkCupid and some of the people I had met were from the dating app. Fed up with all the wasted time, I went in and set my filters very specifically to the type of person I thought I wanted to date, refining everything. Once I hit "Save" on the filters, only one result came up.

The username was a witty play on the person's name, the photos were *adorable*, and the profile was well written (and actually more verbose than mine—a rare thing). I sent over a first message and waited with bated breath.

The person opened the message almost immediately, but didn't reply. That's okay; maybe he had something going on. Roughly three days went by with no reply, so I worked up the courage to send a second message. The second message was also opened nearly immediately and I got a reply a few minutes later. We chatted back and forth on OkCupid for a bit but quickly switched to texting. I was leaving town at the end of the week, so our choice was to go on a date that week or wait nearly two weeks to go on a date. We naturally opted to go on a date sooner rather than later.

We went to Fountainhead, one of my favorite places in Chicago. The date ended up lasting more than five hours (until past 1 a.m.!) because we were having such a good time. He was such a gentleman, too: only the briefest of hugs and we each went on our way. (I later found out that he didn't even realize it was a date. His friends

One Honest Woman

had to enlighten him and then teased him before the remainder of our dates).

Our second and third dates went in similar fashion: The second date was a five-hour foray into deep conversation talking about all manner of things; and the third date lasted more than 11 hours, as we went to a museum, saw a movie, *and* went for dinner and drinks. We leveled up from hugs to forehead kisses, and I found myself touched by his gentlemanly nature.

It quickly became clear that this was working, so on the fourth date, he came home with me to Michigan, where I introduced him to a close friend who in many ways has become a father figure in my life. They had a conversation about a potential relationship between him and I and then we went to the beach. All the major things in my life are tied to bodies of water or the number 7. This particular day was July 7th (7/7), and we were at a beach. This was going to go well, right?

He asked me what I wanted out of life and out of a potential relationship. I took some time to answer, and then he answered the same questions. I'd never been asked such deep questions prior to possibly dating someone before (perhaps this is the lesson in my year of dating errors). By the end of the conversation, it was decided: We were officially dating, and I hadn't even properly kissed the boy.

The next day, we went to Gull Lake with some friends of mine (water, again). The day was a big realization about how much I love water and lakes and boats and all that comes with that. I didn't realize how much I loved it until someone else described it to me from the outside looking in. I was sitting next to him on the boat and he was looking at me with a face of utter adoration. When I asked him what he was doing, he said that he knew I liked water, but seeing how truly and completely happy I was near a body of water was magical.

Shortly after we started dating, I was faced with the decision of moving 300 miles away to take a job at Google. Even though it meant we would be long distance, he championed this decision wholeheartedly—something I had never experienced before. And just a couple months later, I was offered a position on a new

One Honest Woman

team at Google. Without hesitation, he again said, "Go for it," even though it was going to extend the amount of time I would have to be away from Chicago.

He taught me so much—most importantly this: Find someone who supports your happiness, not just simply makes you happy. He and I faced a lot of hard things in our relationship but this mindset of supporting one another's happiness is an important value to have.

This boy also had a life-changing hobby. He takes photos of lamps everywhere he goes. It's a legitimate obsession. There is a Snapchat group and an Instagram account dedicated to this. It's Serious Business. But more than just the goofiness of capturing cool lamps wherever he goes, it's become a reminder for me to stop and breathe. We move so fast in this life, running from meeting to meeting, meal to party, car to home. So much of the experience happens in the in-betweens, but we miss it because we're on the go. Hunting for cool lamps to send along became an unintentional reminder to stop and pause.

Our relationship wasn't meant to last forever, however, and we eventually split up. Though we had many commonalities and shared a lot of the same values, we operated our lives differently, and unfortunately those methodologies clashed. Though that relationship is long over, it taught me this:

Lust is not a substitute for love.

Commitment means only as much as the intentions behind the mouth that offers it.

Definitions are not universal.

The things you think you need are not the things you actually need, and the things you actually need will break you.

Trust is easy to give. It's as simple as closing your eyes and taking a step. But once trust is broken? It's nearly impossible to repair. Be honest with yourself when your faith in someone or something is gone, and don't hang on forever.

Have grace, and be graceful. We as humans make "infinite promises," promises of forever or to always be there. Know that these promises are conditional: "our" forever, or always there except when I can't be. Choose to not hold the conditionality of a promise against someone.

Pain tolerance is situational.

You are a vessel and when your well runs dry, it will take a powerful flood to refill it. Don't let your well run dry.

Every relationship you're in, from the one with your mother to the one with your partner, will be unbalanced—sometimes in your favor, sometimes against. Know your limit of how far the unbalancing can go. Once you determine that limit, set aside your pride and don't hold the imbalance up to that limit against the other person.

Unlearning habits crafted for a specific relationship will take time (and some are better left learned).

People can and will surprise you. The ones you expect the most of will disappoint you, and the ones you expect the least of will become treasured connections. Manage your expectations.

Be afraid to give your all. When it feels right, give your all. But for all that is holy, be afraid to give your all. When you're afraid to give your all, you're a better judge of whom/when to give it.

One person cannot be your everything, even if they promise they can. It is too much for one person to carry.

And perhaps the most powerful thing I've learned: You are an evolving creature, continually changing each day. Trust yourself when your mind says you're open to a new (or old) experience.

But all this isn't to say that moving on is easy.

Moving on.

Those two words are two of the most loaded words in the English language. But what does it mean to move on? When do you know you've done it? Where's the checklist that says you've earned the badge and you can finally sew it to your sash?

There's no right answer. There's no wrong answer, either. It's an individual thing (and honestly, you'll think you've moved on three or four times before you finally manage it).

Have you moved on when you go on the first date afterward?

Have you moved on when it's someone else's lips pressed to your forehead?

Have you moved on when someone new finds all the best places that serve pineapples (pineapple pizza, hot dogs with pineapples, the list goes on) and makes it their mission to take you to every single one? (If you don't like pineapples, my heart aches for you. But I love them.)

Your heart fills up so full that there was no way there was space left, space for harboring that sadness, that disappointment.

And then your blinders finally start to slip away.

When you're with someone, you become blind. It's voluntary; nobody forcefully takes your sight away. But over time, your ability to see the bad in someone, your ability to protect your heart completely—they fade. The more in love and devoted you become, the stronger your blinders become. The things that would have gotten under your skin don't; it's just who they are.

But once you're apart, and your blinders start to fall? Your vision clears. You discover all of these things that you'd become numb to, willfully ignorant of. You stop granting blanket grace and start assigning responsibility. It's part of moving on: understanding what will have to change.

And once those blinders are completely gone? You start to see the full truth. The patterns you didn't see before. The lies you forgave before they were even uttered. The trust that you'd patched up so many times it looked more like a cobblestone pathway than a beautiful Monet.

Moving on is complicated. There's no right way, no wrong way. No time line, no clearly defined start and finish. There isn't a process that you can go through, guaranteeing success if followed to the letter. You just have to trust your heart, be open to your feelings, and breathe. Then begin again.

Beginning again is like lighting a match. You know that moment when you strike a match and you hold your breath as it lights? It's unintentional, subconscious even, but we all do it. That split second as the match head erupts into flames and you feel the power of holding fire in your hands.

That's what moving on is like. You light a match and the fire that results becomes the change.

I've never been the girl who was treated "right" in relationships. I gave my all from the start, as anyone does, but never stepped back when I didn't get someone's all in return. I just kept giving, even as they started closing themselves off.

But when you give without receiving, your vessel empties. Your capacity to care for someone weakens. You become lesser. The power dichotomy in the relationship shifts and not in the good way.

Dannie Lynn Fountain

Beginning again, lighting the match, watching the fire grow—all serve as a reminder that I deserve better and makes me want to be the best for you, too.

> *we are too quick to accept less than we deserve and then blame others when things don't go well. what have you blamed others for? where do you still hold grudges? is it time to be open and let go?*

accidental googler

LEARNING TO TRUST

Accidental Googler

A little more than nine years ago, I took my first client. We worked together and had a great time, and I realized this marketing thing could be a really profitable side hustle. That's all it was ever meant to be.

I side hustled through the rest of high school, through undergrad, while working on my master's, and while working a corporate job. Then, in 2016, I was laid off twice in one year. Instead of gambling on the corporate world some more, I went "full time"—and in some ways, I thought I'd achieved the ultimate pinnacle of success. Doesn't every entrepreneur want to go "full time"?

Here's the thing:

We live in a world that demands perfection. Chases ultimate success. Thirsts for that next tier of recognition. Once I achieved full-time entrepreneurship and thought I'd made it big, the next steps in the ladder appeared, like when you're playing Candy Crush and the cloud cover lifts and you can see the next 20 levels. I started speaking at conferences, garnering press coverage, and upleveling my service offerings. The bar continued to rise.

I'm the girl who's seen the world, gotten a tattoo or 20, survived being broken, and is living her best life.

Shouldn't that be enough? I've been to more countries than I've spent years on this earth. At 24, I've been a part of amazing campaigns that have had profound impact not only on the marketplace but also on individual human lives. I've collaborated with talented people and created and some of the coolest projects.

And yet, the bar still continues to rise. We live in a world that no longer honors strife. We're expected to put our best face on, never share the mess, and never share what's going on. We put out beautiful content on a daily basis, but we never really talk about our struggles. What keeps us up at night.

The one thing people who know me well have always appreciated about me is my willingness to share the mess. Getting caught in foreign countries, narrowly missing terrorist attacks, surviving child abuse, a year of shitty first dates. As a reader of this book, it's as if you've been here for it all.

I started 2017 as a digital nomad, intent on traveling to 50+ cities by the time the year was over. As the year began and the end of Q1 approached, it seemed I was on track to do just that. I flew on more planes in the first quarter of that year than I think I'd ever been on in a full year before that. Throughout the year, I continued to travel and passionately explore the world, and then in late July, an unexpected opportunity fell into my lap. I found myself the accidental interviewee at this little tech company called Google. After three rounds of grueling interviews, I accepted a job offer and officially started on September 18th, nearly a year to the day after my second layoff in 2016.

On September 18, 2017, I re-entered the corporate world unafraid. I finally began to honor the fact that I have always straddled that line. I acknowledged that my skills are best utilized when I am willing to be both entrepreneur and corporate employee. This is a scary journey. I don't know what's going to happen on the other side. I've spent the past nine years building a business, and all of 2017 building it full time, and now I have stepped back into that "side hustler" space and said yes to the corporate world again.

As you read this text, I'm now well into my time at "the big G" (as Granny so lovingly calls it) and, while this may have been an unconventional choice for someone having such an incredibly adventurous year, I am beyond grateful that I made the decision to step back into the corporate world. Never have I been so excited to get up every day and go to work, nor have I ever been challenged so much in a role. Google truly is the corporate version of "the happiest place on earth." My coworkers and I joke that "every

One Honest Woman

day that our badge still works is a good day," but it's so true. There's so much experimentation happening here, I am learning far more about marketing than I ever have.

I stand before you and proudly say, "I work at Google," a sentence I never thought I'd say. Google is too new of an adventure to try and unpack the experience here. As they say, that's a whole other book. But I will say this: Working at Google has taught me that no matter your skill set, and no matter your core talents, there *is* a place that needs the unique blend you bring to the table. You might just have to be patient until you find it.

so what's next?

MOVING FORWARD

So What's Next?

My life thus far has been nothing short of the grandest adventure, 2017 specifically. I cannot even begin to express how much I have enjoyed traveling recently. Every place was a new adventure, and I was finally able to meet so many of my entrepreneurial friends in person. It's a foreign concept to try to explain to someone how a person who has been your "online co-worker" for years plays such a critical role in your life and now you finally get the opportunity to meet them in person.

Getting to spend so much time with Meghan in Nashville; going on an accidental adventure to get tattoos with Devan, Reina, and Sam in

Portland; late-night Whataburger with the women at Illume Retreat in Waco; finally getting to hug Lara in person at C@H in Raleigh; and experiencing intimate moments of deep conversation with so many women the first time we connected in person have been the absolute most joyful parts of this year.

Jenna and I talked about the realities of what "going nomad" really was and what was I trying to escape from; Kat/Rachel and I had a very serious conversation about where faith/Christ/homosexuality all intersected; Meghan and I talked about the realities of life and difficult decisions. None of these conversations would have been possible without this year of travel.

I also think of the "firsts" of 2017. I sit back and wonder how it's possible that there are still "firsts" that exist in my life. But there truly are. From trivial firsts like that first bite of a Voodoo Donuts treat to major firsts like starting a job that I truly believe will become a career, it's been nothing short of earth-shattering. I became a lingerie model this year. Never in a million years did I think that a lingerie brand would ask me not once but *twice* to model their products. I never knew I could look so beautiful. (Leslie, thank you.)

This life has taught me so much, from lessons in what matters most (both in terms of people you build friendships with and things you own) to experiences that have absolutely changed my life. Whether it was the flight that I almost missed in Morocco (because my previous flight was cancelled and Casablanca's taxi system is a chaotic mess) or the first day I used my badge to open a door at Google, I am beyond grateful for this life I lead.

I learned to live with just what I needed. Living out of just a carry on suitcase and a backpack, traveling to multiple cities in the same week—it all means that there's not a lot of room for extra stuff. I learned how to pack a suitcase nice and neatly, maximizing space. I also learned what I really needed and what I didn't need. Many of the things in my suitcase when I first took off in January had been sold or donated by summer, because I hadn't used them in the time they'd spent in my suitcase. I wore the same pair of Tieks for most of 2017, only recently switching to a brand new pair of Rothys when I started at

Google. I also really slimmed down my essentials, combining beauty products and learning to air-dry my hair.

I learned to go with the flow. I'm the kind of person who plans things out way in advance. There's a plan for how I'm going to plan to do things (the word *pre-plan* is appropriate, although it's an oxymoron). I learned to let go and to let the adventures happen as they wanted to.

I learned to say yes to opportunity. There's a lot to be said for 180-degree pivots. I made a couple of those in 2017, the biggest being my decision to take a job at Google. This turned out to be one of the most pivotal experiences of 2017 (no pun intended). I'm now happily back in Corporate America, though Google is analogous to Disney World in many ways. I'm back to the side hustle, back to juggling all the things, and back to learning so much every single day. I also said yes to speaking more than 60 times in 2017 at conferences across the globe, an experience I will never forget. It's been a tremendous adventure getting to make this life a reality.

I learned to ask for help. More than once in

2017, my place to stay vanished at the last minute, a flight was cancelled, or my bank account was frozen. This extended beyond nomad life and eventually became a new habit.

For the first time in my life, I truly understand the phrase *it takes a village.* We cannot exist fully if we live life in a silo and you, my sweet friends and family, are my village. The truth? I have no idea what's next. I would never have imagined that this is what my life would be at the moment, let alone considering what the future is going to be. As soon as I know, I'll tell you!

Acknowledgments

This is the first time I've *truly* written a book by myself. No contributors, no co-authors. Having said that, this book still would not have been possible without the amazing support of some truly incredible people!

First, to my editor, **Jodi Brandon**. Girl, you have put in a tremendous amount of work on this book and I am profoundly grateful to you. From our weekly coaching calls (because y'all know I need accountability to get things done sometimes) to actually reading my flowery and verbose writing, I am grateful for you. This book would not be real, published, or in readers' hands without your hard work and many red pens (or pink Google Docs markups).

A massive thank-you to **those who have challenged me** and what I'm doing. This book wouldn't have been finished without the motivation you offered me to push through my blocks and get my message out there. You taught me that not only is there a market for my story, but there are people who want to hear it, too. I'm so grateful to have found my true tribe. At the end of the day, we are all after the same goal: community over competition. This book aims to stay true to this goal without fail.

To my **incredible cover designer,** Ari of Chykalophia. You knocked it out of the park on the first try, immediately sensing my vision and capturing it visually better than I ever could have. Thank you. Your work is the first and last thing people see about this book; it matters.

To my **beta readers.** Thank you for all your hard work, feedback, and notes. This book improved exponentially from first pass to final print because of your input and dedication throughout the writing process.

To my mom, **Cyndi.** This book launches on the seven-year anniversary of the day you took me in. I could never find the words to sum up everything that you have done for me in this lifetime. You are the reason I am who I am today—the reason I made it through many of the things I tell tales of in this book. You are the reason I have a place to call home, a family that loves me, and roots to keep me grounded. I owe you my life.

To **my entire family,** who supported me through this "crazy idea" of writing a book not once but *four* times, on top of everything else I do in life, thank you. Thank you for being my unofficial editors, my life coaches, my support system, and the people I can always count on.

To **old friends.** You know who you are. You've lived much of the contents of this book side-by-side with me. Thank you for experiencing the crazy and choosing to stick around, and for being the incredible people I love and count on today.

To **new friends.** Whether you met me six months or two years ago, you've had an impact on my life. You've become people I share many of my secrets with and people who are there for me whenever I need anything and for generally being incredible souls.

To **Joey, Sam, Caitlyn, Sarah, Mariel, Alex, Helen,** and anyone else who has held me while I cried, talked me off ledges, rescued me, pulled splinters from my feet, let me crash on couches, etc. You're the real deal.

To **Class Togepi.** Y'all are honestly the best bunch of coworkers I have ever had. I really feel like we *are* a family. You guys are so good about checking in on me, including me, even FaceTiming me into team events when I can't be there because of work or a conference. I'm beyond grateful for all of you.

To **everyone who was mentioned** in this book, named or otherwise. Thank you for being a part of my life, positive or negative. My interactions and experiences with you made my story (and this book) what it is today.

To **every boss I've ever had**, good or bad. I'm sure it isn't easy to manage someone with entrepreneurial dreams. I'm sure it's no small feat to let me travel the globe while still delivering quality results for you and the company. Thank you for your patience and grace.

To **those who entered and exited my life** over the course of this book. This book is nearly three years in the making. In that time, I have made friends, lost friends, fallen in and out of love, and met and left coworkers. I grateful for those of you who passed through my life during this time. Whether we met and parted ways over the course of the past three years or you simply moved on to bigger and better things, I am thankful for the influence you had on my life.

To my **LE Consulting team** (especially Caitlyn), for tolerating all the overlap between LEPC and this book. For taking on a bigger burden because I am spread so thin. For continuing to be my OG book customers and dear friends.

To the **Baller Biz Chicks** and the **BFF Mastermind** squads. Y'all are the realest. I am lucky to have two of the best mastermind groups on the planet, I don't know what I'd do without you keeping me sane.

To **my clients,** for knowing and honoring the fact that I was writing a book while working with you and loving me anyway. You are amazing, each and every one of you!

And finally to **you, my readers.** My journey has been a whirlwind. I stand here, a mid-20s girl, and say to you that you have so much life to live, no matter what you've experienced thus far. Believe in your story; understand the truth of your experience. Know that you have worth, because sometimes we all forget that.

About the Author

Dannie Lynn Fountain is a marketing strategist and whip-smart whiskey drinker. Currently working at Google, Dannie honed her skills working in marketing for brands such as Whirlpool and H&R Block. She has a combined nine years experience as an entrepreneur and strategist. Today, she works with entrepreneurs and corporate clients alike to brainstorm, strategize, and implement strategic marketing processes to better their business and increase their sales. Beyond strategy, Dannie is the author of four books on entrepreneurship and a regular speaker on strategy worldwide. Her work and the work of teams she has been a part of has been submitted to and recognized by Cannes Lions, the Effies, & more.

Website: www.danniefountain.com
Podcast: www.sidehustlegal.com
Speaking: www.dannielynnfountain.com

Made in the USA
Las Vegas, NV
18 March 2023